Penguin Handbooks
The Pip Book

Keith Mossman was born in Barnet, Hertfordshire, in
1913, the son of a farmer. He worked in agriculture and
as a private gardener in a variety of jobs, and also as a
single-handed market gardener for ten years. He was
a freelance journalist intermittently from the age of
eighteen and concentrated on full-time writing when forced
to retire from outdoor work in the late 1960s because
of ill-health. He had a lifelong interest in plant
physiology and behaviour as well as in practical aspects of
horticulture. Keith Mossman died in 1979.

Among his many publications are *Looking Forward to
Retirement* (1971), *The Kitchen Garden* (1972), *The
Garden Room* (1973), *Growing, Freezing and Cooking*
(with Mary Norwak; 1974), *Make Money from Garden
Produce* (1975), *Indoor Light Gardening* (1976), *Home
Grown* (1977), *Vegetable Gardening* (1977) and *The
English Countryside* (1977). He has also made substantial
literary contributions to *The Country Book* and *The
Second Country Book* (edited by Barbara Hargreaves).

KEITH MOSSMAN

The Pip Book

Line Drawings by Marion Bagshawe

Penguin Books

Penguin Books Ltd, Harmondsworth,
Middlesex, England
Penguin Books, 625 Madison Avenue,
New York, New York 10022, U.S.A.
Penguin Books Australia Ltd, Ringwood,
Victoria, Australia
Penguin Books Canada Ltd, 2801 John Street,
Markham, Ontario, Canada L3R 1B4
Penguin Books (N.Z.) Ltd, 182–190 Wairau Road,
Auckland 10, New Zealand

First published by H. F. & G. Witherby 1973
Published in Penguin Books 1977
Reprinted 1978 (twice), 1979, 1981

Made and printed in Great Britain by
Richard Clay (The Chaucer Press) Ltd, Bungay, Suffolk
Set in Linotype Pilgrim

Contents

Introduction

I wonder if it would grow?

The question must have occurred to everyone looking at a pip or seed or stone among the household debris, but usually it's no more than a passing thought, to be discarded with the pips themselves. Just occasionally it may be followed by another: Would it grow into something worth having? And a third: How do I set about growing it?

The honest answer to the first two is: Quite possibly. The answers to the third are rather varied, and I have tried to set some of them down in this little book.

We nearly all know of people who have grown avocado or orange or peach trees from their seeds, but they all too often seem unable to tell us how they did it. They sometimes imply that by some Topsyesque process the thing just growed. But when *we* try it just doesn't.

Meanwhile, things are lying around that would develop into attractive house plants given half a chance, and only the odd lucky individual is preparing to pick mandarin oranges from the tree that cost nothing but a pip and patience. Many of the subjects raised from throwaway materials have a decorative value equal to that of any conventional indoor plant; their botanical interest is frequently greater and their cost in money terms invariably less.

But the production of cut-price exotics is not the whole story. Indoor gardening has progressed far beyond the purchase and tending of mature plants. The aim now is increasingly to grow your own thing, to experiment, to try something different. Here are some things not found in every florist's window, but which one can, so to speak, rescue from the dustbin or steal from the shopping basket. 'Market-basket gardening', the Americans call it, and its fascination lies not only in the strangeness and beauty of some of its end products but in what it can teach one about plants.

The pips among the peelings, the conkers and acorns brought home from a walk in the park, come with no guarantees and no instructions, yet they can be a rich gardening legacy for those willing to 'have a go'. Information on some of these plants is not readily available, and the hints on their culture given here are sometimes no more than a sound basis for personal experiment.

I believe most of the experiments will work, though if you succeed by ignoring every bit of advice in the following pages I would be delighted to hear about it. And, after a lifetime of messing about with plants, not in the least surprised.

K.M.

1 Turning Pips into Plants

The general care of house plants is now pretty well understood. We all have plants of some sort in the home, and the knowledge we sometimes lack at the beginning is apt to come with various harrowing experiences as we go along. Instruction on indoor plants, though, does tend to concentrate on the day-to-day management of the full-grown specimens that we buy, or with which we are presented. We seem to get much less information on how to raise them from seed or cuttings, and this is a very different proposition. As different as housekeeping for adults is to looking after a baby.

Of course, one learns far more about plants and their peculiarities by propagating them at home than by the routine attentions given to fully matured ones. It's a lot more trouble but a great deal more interesting. It transforms the simple idea of decoration into the absorbing hobby of indoor gardening.

Like other hobbies this one can be pursued expensively or economically; this book is heavily on the side of economy, being entirely concerned with producing beautiful plants from unwanted materials.

The fact that one is dealing with a variety of discarded pips and other oddments, great as their potentialities are, means that all one's efforts are something of a gamble as well as a test of skill. If you buy a packet of seeds they will have been tested for certain minimum standards of germination; failure with them will be the fault of the grower. No such guarantee can be given for the pips saved from your orange or the coffee beans from the grocers. The best that can be said is that they probably *are* fertile, and that *given the right treatment* they will produce fascinating results at little cost other than some time and trouble.

All gardeners know that there are many different ways of doing things, all equally successful. They also know that in the cultivation of every plant there are one or two basic rules which just cannot be ignored. This, I think, is where a lot of aspiring pip-growers come unstuck. There is no packet with printed instructions and not much guidance to be found in books. Some evidence, direct or hearsay, is always available about the friend with a marvellous grapefruit tree – 'I just stuck a pip in and it grew' – but this is no sort of help to the many who have stuck pips in and they haven't grown. A completely hit-or-miss approach is always going to score more misses than hits.

If the pips or seeds are infertile there is nothing to be done about it but to try again. But if given reasonable conditions, a fair percentage of pips may be expected to germinate, the important thing being to know what any particular pip considers reasonable. For instance, much of the fruit we eat is of tropical or subtropical origin and its seeds will be designed to germinate in steamy heat, lying in decaying vegetation and drenched by warm rain. You can hardly expect them to come to life in rather dry soil in a cool living room.

Again, you may collect handfuls of acorns and chestnuts during autumn walks, bring them home and plant them immediately indoors, only to find that they lie sullen and dormant for months on end with no vestige of a shoot. Yet there's nothing wrong with them, they are just *meant* to stay like that, exposed to the rigours of winter, before being ready to respond to the warmth of spring. The difference between success and failure in the fascinating business of pip-begotten plants so often depends on knowing these odd individual habits.

GROWING FROM SEED INDOORS

Indoor gardening is much easier than it used to be, thanks to the wide range of easy-to-use products available in every garden shop. The initial requirements of the pip-grower are really very modest, and the purpose of this chapter is to suggest the least messy, least time-consuming ways of going about things.

If you possess a heated greenhouse or conservatory and experience of gardening under glass all this is of no interest to you, but I'm assuming that, like most house plant enthusiasts, you have to manage with the facilities of the ordinary home. That is, some sunny windows, a comfortable average temperature in winter, and some source of a little extra heat like an airing cupboard or a shelf over a storage heater. These are the essentials for all indoor gardening; materials and equipment are largely a matter of choice.

Light

Adequate light is vital to all green-leaved plants; without it they cannot absorb the carbon dioxide from the air and convert it into solid tissues by the process of photosynthesis. Plants differ greatly in the amount of light they need; some, like many ferns, are used to living in dark, shady places, but nearly all flowering plants require a lot of light and some direct sunlight.

Young seedlings suffer from lack of light more quickly than mature plants. They get a starting push from the nutrients stored in the seed but then they have to build up their own tissues very quickly, an impossibility without light. In a poorly-lighted position they shoot up in an attempt to reach more light, becoming 'drawn' and spindly. This effect is even worse when the environment is warm and growth is rapid; greenhouse enthusiasts know that temperature and light must be kept in balance – that more heat is permissible when daylight increases. Some of the things to be raised from pips must, as we have already noted, have a high temperature to germinate. Alright, start them in the airing cupboard if that's the hottest spot, *but bring them into the light as soon as shoots emerge from the compost*. Not immediately into bright sunlight but into a warm and rather shaded place for a few days first.

Light is equally necessary for the rooting of cuttings. A cutting is simply a piece of a plant which has to remain alive while forming roots for a completely independent existence. To do this it must have warmth and moisture, but also light. A cutting kept in the dark will simply die.

Warmth and Humidity

The ideal place for germinating seeds, for seedlings, or cuttings, is a propagator. Innumerable versions of this handy gadget are available, and homemade substitutes are easy to concoct.

A propagator is simply a transparent container in which pots or seed trays may be enclosed. It may have its own electric heating unit, or be without internal heating and dependent on the warmth of the room. The value of a heated propagator is obvious; kept close to a light window you can start all types of seeds and cuttings in it. An unheated one is also valuable, it maintains a close, humid atmosphere, reduces the frequency of watering, and protects seedlings from cold draughts and wild fluctuations of temperature. In fact, a propagator simplifies the whole business of plant raising.

The most elementary of home-made propagators is a jam jar. Place a few crocks or pebbles at the bottom for drainage, then a few inches of compost. Drop in one or two seeds or pips, add a covering layer of compost, water gently, and cover the top with a piece of polythene secured by an elastic band. This can stand on the mantelpiece or near the cooker and will need only a little water about once a week. Its great disadvantage, apart from its very limited capacity, is the difficulty of getting the seedlings out undamaged – one either has to dig them out with a table fork while still tiny or lay the jar on its side and crack it open with a smart blow from a hammer delivered near the base.

A better proposition than the jam jar is the polythene bag. The seeds are sown or cuttings inserted in a fairly large half-pot, which is then placed at the bottom of a bag plenty big enough to accommodate it. The bag is brought together at the top and tightly clipped or tied. Provided as much air as possible has been enclosed, so that the bag is ballooned out, it will stand up and not collapse on the emergent seedlings. This is a very efficient and easily transportable mini-propagator, especially if placed over a source of heat. The shelf of an electric storage heater – not the top of the heater itself – is excellent. The degree of bottom heat can be regulated by standing the enclosed pot on varying thicknesses of newspaper.

A larger DIY propagator can be made by covering the top of a wooden box with glass or polythene, and this can be heated by arranging a length of soil-warming cable in a series of loops at the bottom and covering it with a layer of granulated peat on which pots can stand. Soil-warming cables are inexpensive to buy and operate, but like all electrical appliances, must be installed and used as the manufacturers advise.

If you decide to buy a propagator the unheated form is likely to be a rigid transparent plastic cover or 'dome', fitted over a metal or plastic tray. These are usually made narrow enough to stand on a window sill and admit the maximum of light to their occupants. A simple heated form, the Humex 'Pottagator' for instance, is only about eight inches wide with an area equal to that of an ordinary seed tray. With a loading of 16 watts it would not cost more than three pence a week to run. Larger models in the same range, thermostatically controlled and with room for a number of pots and trays, will cost no more than eight pence a week for current.

Summing up: seeds must have warmth and moisture to germinate; seedlings must also have these things, plus abundant light; vegetative propagation such as the growing of pineapple plants from the crowns of fruit requires a moist atmosphere not easily obtainable in a living room. The easiest way to achieve these conditions and to protect tender seedlings from draughts and all the other hazards of living with humans is to use a propagator. No matter how simple.

Composts

In this book the word means the special soils for growing plants in pots. Such a soil must have certain qualities. It must contain a certain minimum of plant foods, it must be well drained, and it should be obtainable in small quantities and easy to handle. Two main types of compost may be bought at every garden shop, the loam-based and the soil-less.

Loam-based composts are composed of sterilised soil, peat, sand, and balanced fertilisers. The most reliable are those in the John Innes range, which are sold in four grades. The seed compost (JI Seed) is used for sowing, the seedlings being transferred to the various potting composts (JIP 1, JIP 2, or JIP 3). The only difference between these three is the amount of fertiliser used in them. No. 1 has the least and is suitable for small or relatively short-lived plants and for the initial potting-up of seedlings. The other two are richer in nutrients and are employed for larger, fast-growing plants and for shrubs which are grown in large containers and only infrequently repotted.

Two points about the John Innes composts must be emphasised. They are *not* a standardised proprietary product; they are made up according to the formulas worked out by the John Innes Institute many years ago, but even if the manufacturer keeps faithfully to the recipe the finished product will vary enormously with the quality of the soil he uses. Another thing to remember is that the composts will not store indefinitely owing to the breakdown of the chemical nutrients; they should be used within six months of purchase.

Soil-less composts have proved a blessing to horti-culture and especially to the indoor gardener. They contain – as the name implies – no soil whatever, consisting of special grades of peat reinforced with plant foods. They are very light, clean to handle, can be bought in large or small quantities, and in my experience give consistently good results. Perhaps this is because they are so consistent in their make-up. I would certainly recommend them for most of the plants mentioned in this book.

We need not go into the various brand names under which soil-less composts are sold. All those produced by well-known manufacturers are good, though you will find certain differences in them. Some are sold in specific grades for seed-sowing, taking cuttings, and potting older plants. Others are supplied as a single all-purpose compost. A few points should be remembered when using these convenient mixtures:

Read the instructions that come with them. Then write to the makers asking if they can supply you with fuller information. Most of the larger companies provide very useful leaflets on their products, and you can pick up valuable cultural tips from them.

Soil-less composts are sold in plastic bags and in a slightly moist condition. Retain this moisture by always folding the top of the bag over after use.

When sowing, fill the flower pot or seed pan to the brim with compost and press it down gently with the fingers. This leaves it some distance below the rim of the container. Level the surface and sow the pips on it, covering them with more compost to the required depth. Water carefully and never let the compost get dry enough to turn a light brown on the surface. In small peat pots, where the aim is to produce single plants, a small group of pips or seeds is sown in the centre. After germination the seedlings are reduced to one as quickly as possible.

Soil-less potting composts contain enough plant food for about two months growth without additional feeding. After that time liquid fertiliser may have to be given, depending on the season and the rate at which the plant is growing. It is often quite happy in soil-less compost through the winter months without extra feeding.

Foster homes for pips. This is the supremely lazy way of sowing in which you make use of pots and compost already occupied by house plants. You can plant quite a lot of pips this way without appreciable effort whenever you happen to notice vacant spaces. There is no sense of grievance when the majority don't grow and a feeling of collecting a bonus when a few of them do.

The snags are these: You must use only the pots of plants kept in a warm room, and only those which have an area of bare compost encircling the plant. The pot must be watered frequently – it's no good popping pips in alongside a cactus that will be watered once a month. Very large stones are usually out of place; don't use this method for avocados or chestnuts but for the smaller seeds like orange or lemon pips.

Plant close to the pot rim, not too deep, and after a few weeks keep a look-out for any emerging seedlings. They must be removed and potted up individually as soon as the seed leaves are clear of the ground. To wait until they get larger means more disturbance both for them and the pot's main occupants.

CUTTINGS

Propagation by cuttings is not all that important to the pip-grower, though its principles also apply to other kinds of 'vegetative propagation' such as the rooting of pineapple tops. Some of the plants we shall consider, the coffee tree for instance, can be multiplied more quickly by the successful rooting of cuttings than by raising new ones from scratch, so a knowledge of the subject can sometimes be useful.

A cutting is a detached piece of a plant which has to be kept alive until it can form roots and set up on its own. To do this it must have the same sort of environment as germinating seed, but rather more so. It must be kept warm, moist, and in the light. The air surrounding it must be humid to reduce the loss of moisture from the leaves, for if the cutting loses all the fluid from its cells it will die. It must also be planted in a soil – the 'rooting medium' which can be kept moist without becoming waterlogged and airless.

Taking the Cutting

The stem or tip cutting is the type most often used. It consists of about three inches from the tip of a main stem or a lateral, usually cut just *below* a leaf joint. The bottom leaves are removed and the cut surface is dipped in a rooting powder. This is a synthetic hormone which encourages the cut tissues to heal and dormant root cells to develop; a small tin of it lasts for years and it is often a considerable help in persuading difficult subjects to get themselves rooted.

Other forms of cuttings are sometimes used, including the leaf and leaf-stalk, and the leaf-bud, which consists of a very short section of stem bearing a single leaf. The end of the section is inserted into the growing medium and the dormant bud in the leaf axil grows into a new stem. This method is often used for climbing plants whose long stems can be divided into a number of cuttings.

Other forms of vegetative reproduction may occasionally be useful to the experienced pipster.

Offsets are sucker-like growths which appear at the base of a plant, from which they can be detached and potted up. The pineapple will sometimes oblige with several simultaneously. *Layering* is the rooting of a branch *before* removing it from the parent plant. A shallow slanting cut is made on the underside of the branch close to a leaf joint, this part then being pegged down on a pot of moist compost which just covers it. If the branch refuses to be tethered to a pot you can surround the cut portion with a handful of damp soil-less compost covered with polythene. This is tied tightly at both ends so that the branch appears to be growing through a short, fat sausage.

Rooting Mediums

Soil-less composts are as good as anything, though I like to add a little coarse sand to improve drainage. Coarse sand – sometimes called 'grit' is usually better than silver sand for this purpose, and indeed for all soil mixtures.

Pure sand is also excellent for rooting cuttings, though as it is a sterile medium with no plant food in it the cuttings must be transferred to an ordinary compost as soon as they are rooted. An even better material of this sort is *vermiculite*, a form of mica which has been heated and exploded into small flakes. It is very light and clean and holds moisture while remaining open and porous. A cutting in vermiculite soon develops a tremendous root system, but again must be transplanted to a normal compost.

A very different rooting medium is provided by the Jiffy 7, described under 'Pots and Potting'. A cutting rooted in this labour-saving little invention can be allowed to grow on vigorously for several weeks before being potted up.

Treatment of Cuttings

Except when the Jiffy 7 is used, cuttings are best grown in a small pot or half-pot. Fill it to within an inch of the top with the rooting medium and insert the cuttings round the outside, close to the rim. The pot, which must have a drainage hole, is then placed in a propagator.

Here the polythene bag is as good as anything if you have a warm and reasonably light place in which to stand it. Lower the pot into it, preceded if possible by a small saucer – surplus water looks untidy swishing about in the bag – and tie the top very tightly. If properly sealed the cuttings will not need watering more than once a week, and then merely a sprinkle to maintain the general dampness. Signs of growth will prove that rooting has taken place, though if your curiosity is uncontrollable you will not do a cutting any harm by digging it up for inspection. Don't be impatient, cuttings of some evergreen species may take many weeks to root and as long as they are still obviously alive you should carry on tending them.

POTS AND POTTING

Indoor plants raised from seed are going to need pots of different sizes at different times in their lives. An orange pipling will start life in a 3″ pot, but in a few years a 12″ one will be required for the impressive young tree.

Plants should never be 'over-potted', it wastes valuable space on your window sill to have them in pots larger than necessary, and the plant usually thrives best when its roots just comfortably occupy all the compost in the pot.

Pots: Sorts and Sizes

The conventional pot is made of earthenware or of plastic. The latter is rapidly superseding the old-fashioned 'clay' and there are good reasons for this. Plastic pots are much lighter than clays, less easily broken, and because they are non-porous the plants in them need less frequent watering. On the other hand, the porosity of the clay pot means that the compost is less likely to get waterlogged and sour, and the terracotta surface of the earthenware is attractive in appearance as many a decorative container.

Two warnings: New clay pots must be soaked for some hours before use; they absorb a lot of water and if this is not done they will keep the compost perpetually dry. Plastic pots have one disadvantage when used with soil-less compost – the entire set-up is so light that a heavy plant like a vigorous avocado becomes top-heavy. The remedies are either to place the pot in a fairly solid pot-holder or container, or to put a thick layer of sand at the bottom of the pot before planting. The extra weight at this point makes all the difference to the plant's stability.

Peat pots are most useful for the initial sowings and plantings. They are made of compressed peat or peat and wood pulp impregnated with plant food. Not being intended to last for long they are mostly in small sizes, are sometimes square in shape to economise in space, and can be bought in small quantities at all garden shops. Their greatest value is in permitting transplantation with no disturbance to the plant; the roots grow through the pot sides and plant, pot and all, is planted in a larger container with no possibility of a check.

The newest development in peat pots is the compressed block, a boon to the amateur with too little storage room for conventional pots and compost. The Jiffy 7, for instance, consists of a hard disc about the diameter of an old penny. It is sold in convenient packs which include plastic trays with shallow recesses into which the discs are fitted. When soaked in water the discs swell up into two-inch-high columns of fertilised compost, held firmly together by fine netting. On the top of this little column you then sow your pip or insert your cutting, leaving the resultant plant to grow until its roots poke through the netting sides. Growth in these compost blocks is excellent, and a pack containing the equivalent of forty compost-filled pots and their special trays takes up little more storage space than this book.

Potting up and Repotting

The first move of a pipling from its place of germination to a more adult pot should be done with care.

If it started in a peat pot there will be no problems. Simply plant the peat pot in a somewhat larger ordinary pot and the seedling's roots will spread out as the former disintegrates.

When a seedling has to be lifted and replanted this should be done as soon after germination as possible. Anyone who raises bedding plants knows that 'pricking out' from the seed tray is best performed as soon as the seedlings are big enough to handle. Seedlings should be lifted with as much compost as possible round their roots, and always held by the seed-leaves. The stem of a seedling is easily bruised by handling and this can prove fatal.

Plant the young seedling in a small pot, leaving the compost surface at least half an inch below the rim for easy watering. If particularly good drainage is essential a few crocks or pebbles are placed at the bottom of the pot before filling it with compost. 'Crocks' are the fragments of broken clay flower pots, now becoming a rarity with the increasing use of the plastic article. Broken cups and saucers come in useful here, the most effective drainage being obtained from curved pieces placed concave side downwards.

The repotting of mature plants may be necessary annually if they are in soil-less compost, and any plant or shrub must be repotted if seriously pot-bound. One exception to this is the *bonsai* tree, whose roots are always kept closely confined to balance its artificially dwarfed top.

The signs that a plant needs more room are the appearance of roots through the drainage hole and on the surface of the compost, pale or yellowing leaves, and a general look of 'standing still' when it ought to be growing strongly.

The best time for repotting is usually spring or early summer, when there is a quick recovery from the move. Deciduous trees should always be repotted in winter when they are leafless and dormant. Make sure that the plant to be moved is not dry at the roots, and then knock it out of the pot. To do this you hold it upside down, with the pot resting on the palm of the hand and the plant projecting downwards between the fingers. Knock the rim of the pot smartly on the edge of a table or bench and the plant will be loosened enough to slide out easily. The removal of a sturdy orange tree from a 9" pot may not be as easy as this. The safest method here is to lay the pot on its side, grasp the tree firmly around the stem, near the base, and rap the top of the pot rim, first on one side and then on the other, with a mallet or a block of wood.

Loosen any matted roots on the outside of the soil

ball, but don't attempt to shake off too much of the old compost. The new pot should be only one size larger than the old one, and you put enough compost in the bottom to bring the plant up to the right level. Then stand it in a central position and feed the compost slowly down the sides, occasionally tapping the pot to make it settle evenly. Finish off by pressing it firmly down round the outside.

WATERING AND FEEDING

Correct watering of plants in containers is not a matter of rules, of giving everything so much water every so often. It is more an art which has to be learnt by observation.

Go by the look of the compost, the weight of the pot, and the appearance of the plant. Remember that a plant whose pot is crowded with roots will dry out quickly and suffer if not watered frequently. Whereas one whose roots do not fill the pot must be watered very carefully lest the compost becomes soggy and waterlogged and the roots die for lack of oxygen.

A plant in full growth needs more water than one which is dormant or just marking time; one which is in a definite rest period, especialy a deciduous tree in winter, should have only enough to keep the compost moist. The temperature, the dryness of the air, and the climate of the plant's natural habitat, are all things which one has to take into account.

The symptoms of under-watering, flagging foliage, drooping stem, falling leaves and flower buds, are always obvious. But if leaves turn yellow and drop, and the plant looks sickly when the compost is obviously wet, you are probably erring in the opposite direction. Commonsense and an open eye for the first signs of trouble are more valuable than two handfuls of 'green fingers'.

Feeding is necessary when conditions are right for rapid growth, and the food reserves in the compost are running out. It is never essential in the first two or three months after repotting in a soil-less mixture, or the first six to twelve months in JI Potting.

Liquid feeds are now generally used for indoor plants, and they must always be applied as the makers advise. Never try to give a plant an extra boost by using a stronger liquid, keep to the proper dilution and feed more often. And never give liquid fertiliser to a plant that is bone dry; give it a thorough soaking and apply the fertiliser the next day.

2 Three from the Tropics

Two of them are very decorative, and one is attractively odd.

Avocado stones are germinated by many people who then fail to make use of a potentially beautiful indoor evergreen. Date stones are rarely planted because of a widespread conviction that they 'won't grow', yet the feathery-fronded date palm is a house plant worth the trouble of getting it started. The little peanut plant is nice to have around, because it enables you to score off people who think peanuts come from a peanut tree.

THE AVOCADO

The Avocado or Alligator Pear – Persea *gratissima* to those who like to know these things – was introduced to this country as a greenhouse shrub as long ago as 1739. It came originally from the West Indies, but the best commercial varieties are probably those now grown in Florida and California. Gastronomically, I have always thought it grossly over-rated and over-priced, but as long as someone in the family likes the thing there is always the prospect of growing some fine indoor evergreens.

The stone of the avocado is technically known as a 'pit'. Like the fruit itself it is very large, but of course not always fertile. A stone from a fully ripe fruit is said to be the most likely to germinate, and only fully ripe ones are ready to be eaten. The test for ripeness is the same as for an ordinary pear – press the fruit gently at the stem end; if it gives to the pressure it is ripe. It is not advisable to apply this test to the avocados displayed in the fruiterers unless you are prepared to buy the lot or risk an action for wilful damage.

Planting

Soak the stone for forty eight hours, keeping the water tepid if possible by standing the container on a radiator or a hot tank. Don't try to strip away the outer skin unless it seems to be peeling off naturally. The use of tepid water, recommended for soaking all hard pips and stones, is particularly important with a tropical subject like the avocado; germination can be impaired or delayed by a long soak in really cold water.

It is vital that the stone should be planted right way up, and when it is roughly the same shape as the fruit this presents no difficulty. The broad part is the base from which comes the root, and the shoot emerges from the pointed tip. Occasionally the stone is a perfect oval and then the only difference is that the base will be wrinkled and the tip smooth.

Germination in water. This has always been a favourite method with avocado growers. If successful, it enables you to watch the early development of the seedling, and if the seed happens to be a dud you get fairly early warning of the fact from the smell and cloudiness of the water. This may save you several weeks of wasted care and attention.

The base of the stone must be just submerged in the water, which is topped up to keep it at that level. There must be a reasonable depth of water below the stone for the root to expand into when

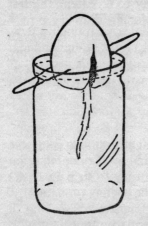

Avocado stone supported by hairpins in water-filled jam jar first stage of germination. Note water-level just above base of stone.

growth starts, and there must be some way of supporting the stone in the right position. The use of the familiar 'hyacinth glass' is one possibility, but the stone may be too small and drop through the opening, or the wrong shape, so that it continually capsizes.

An ordinary jam jar is satisfactory if the stone is to be kept in a fairly dark place like an airing cupboard until the emergence of the shoot, which happens quite a bit after that of the root. The root should not be exposed to more light than necessary and a semi-opaque plastic beaker or tumbler is best if the germinating stone is to be in a normally-lighted room.

The stone is suspended in the receptacle by four toothpicks or sharpened matchsticks pushed a little way into it and resting on the rim. A couple of hairpins, slightly opened out, are equally good and perhaps easier to insert. These supports must not be shoved deep into the stone – just far enough to stay there and hold it up. The sketches illustrate the general arrangement and show the level at which the water is maintained. Slightly warm water is used for the regular topping up and a surrounding temperature of about 70° F (21°C) must be maintained. Unless you have a heated propagator this may entail germinating your avocados in the colder months of the year, when there will be some consistently warm corner over or near a radiator or storage heater. Or, of course, the airing cupboard can be used provided the young plant is not left in the dark once the shoot has appeared.

Germination may take anything from ten days to four or five weeks, and temperature is an important factor in this. Some older greenhouse books, describing the avocado as a 'stove' (hothouse) shrub, recommend a starting temperature of 85°F (30°C), but this is impracticable and unnecessary. Another thing influencing germination time is the stone's state of readiness. Sometimes, especially from a very ripe fruit, it may have a split or gap down the centre and even show signs of the developing embryo inside. A stone in this condition will usually throw out roots and a shoot very quickly if its environment is right, but even the hardest and most unproductive-looking specimen will eventually come to life if you keep it warm and have patience. The time to throw it away and try again is when the base of the stone discolours and the water becomes offensive.

Germination in compost. Either a soil-less or JI potting compost may be used. Seeds of this size and vigour don't need a seed compost, and if, say, Levington Potting or JIP 2 is employed in a 4½" pot the seedlings may be left to grow for a time without potting on.

The stone is planted, blunt end down of course, so that half of it is above the surface. The compost

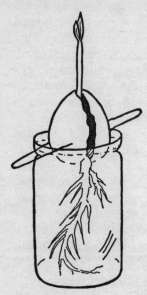

Avocado shoot emerging.

must be made firm around it. Soak before planting and keep the pot warm and moist. If no other propagator is available, enclose it in a plastic bag kept in a really warm corner.

As you will be unable to see the root, the first sign of germination will be the splitting of the stone and the popping up of one or more stems topped with tufts of leaves. You now have a quick-growing young plant to look after.

Growing On

Plants germinated in water should be transferred to pots when the root has developed into quite a large well-branched mass. Use a 4½″ pot and a soilless potting compost which is light and will not damage the more fragile roots. Hold the plant by the

First step in avocado pruning. Top of the shoot has been nipped off and a lateral is developing into a new and less rampant stem.

Avocado transferred to pot. Stone not quite covered by compost.

seed, which is kept with its tip about level with the pot rim, and sift the compost down among the roots, firming it gently with the fingers. Finish up with the top half of the stone above the compost, which must be far enough down to permit easy watering.

There is no desperate hurry to transfer the seedling from water to compost. It can be allowed to grow until the jar or beaker is almost full of roots, especially if you want to stop the young shoot before making the move – a procedure almost unique to the avocado to which we shall come in a moment. The plant never seems to suffer from living on water for several weeks, apparently drawing on the nutrients stored in the enormous seed.

The 4½" pot is a useful size for the avocado's early days, taking up relatively little space on a window sill, but when this tropical tree gets into its stride a move to a larger pot standing on the floor will be imperative. So will the pruning necessary to produce an attractive leafy evergreen shrub.

The first stage in this pruning comes soon after the appearance of the shoot. Several shoots may in fact emerge from the slit in the stone but here we are concerned with the main one which grows very rapidly and is obviously going to form the trunk of the tree. The subsidiary ones may flourish, which will be all to the good, or they may die back, which will not be a disaster.

When the main shoot reaches a height of six inches the top is snipped off a third of the way up, leaving a bare stem about four inches long. The tuft of leaves will have been at the top, so they will have been sacrificed and the main shoot will be leafless. Any side-shoots should be left to grow on naturally.

The object of this operation is to restrict the avocado's urge to throw up an ever-lengthening stem

Avocado stem supported by cane and stopped at required height. Lateral branches forming.

at the expense of everything else. The root system will build up more quickly and the entire habit of the plant will be changed, becoming less of a tree and nearer to the bushy shape needed in an indoor plant.

For a week or so after stopping the stem will show no sign of further growth and you may begin to wonder if you've killed the seedling. Then a new shoot will break from it, more fully clothed with leaves than the original, and this will form the foundation of your indoor shrub.

Repotting and Pruning

The plant will outgrow its 4½" pot in a few
months and should be moved to a 10" one or a small
tub. This will be its permanent home, and to avoid a
yearly repotting it should be planted in JIP 2 instead
of a soil-less compost. There is no objection to the
latter, but it becomes exhausted more quickly than
the loam-based composts when used for large strong-
growing plants. Also, as we have already noticed, it
is so light that a tall plant growing in it is easily
toppled over unless the container is very solid.

Repotting is best done in the spring, but the initial
move to a large pot must be made whenever the
young shrub shows signs of becoming pot-bound.
The appearance of roots from the drainage hole or
on the surface of the compost, the slowing down of
growth and yellowing or even dropping of the
leaves, are signs that a move is urgent. Knock the
plant out and repot it as described in Chapter 1. This
will need a little care as the avocado will now probably be at least two feet high. The soil ball should
be left intact and the roots undisturbed. After repotting stand it in a cool shady place for a couple of
weeks, keeping it well watered.

With the young tree, shrub, or whatever you
choose to call it, settled in a permanent home, you
will have to train it to the size and shape you want.
The aim should be something well-branched, not too
tall, and thickly hung with the great, dark green
glossy leaves – sometimes a foot long – that make it
such a wonderful foliage plant.

Of course, if you have a room with a large vacant,
well-lit wall space you can let your avocado go up
to the ceiling and attain a six foot spread, which it
will do in about three years, given a large enough
container for its roots. However, trees of that size

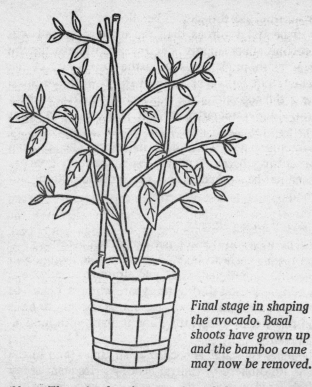

Final stage in shaping the avocado. Basal shoots have grown up and the bamboo cane may now be removed.

(Note: The six drawings are intended as a complete sequence from germination to the established plant. The avocado was chosen for this because of its generally spectacular appearance.)

are unwelcome in an average room, and to have too much space occupied by a single plant is boring. So keep the avocado within bounds.

The stem which grew after the initial stopping may itself have to be stopped when it reaches the maximum height you can permit; just nip out the soft growing point. If a secondary shoot has broken from the base this should be allowed to grow on; it will be less vigorous than the main stem and will probably flop slightly sideways, so improving the general shape. Laterals from the lower part of the main stem should be allowed to grow, while those near the top should be pinched back. You want a roughly pyramidal form, but above all you want young shoots and lots of leaves, not an assembly of bare sticks with a leaf here and there. The stopping or cutting back of unruly or unwanted branches need not be shirked; it does the avocado nothing but good.

General Management

The avocado doesn't need high temperatures except in its earliest stages. A comfortable living room warmth suits it very well, and although it may have a resting period during the year, when it ceases to produce new leaves and shoots, this appears to have no relation to temperature and to vary with individual plants.

Plenty of water is needed at all times, and in the dry atmosphere of central heating a frequent spray with tepid water, and an occasional sponging of the leaves to remove dust is an effective beauty treatment.

A fortnightly feed with liquid fertiliser when the plant is growing strongly is advisable, especially if the plant has been in the same compost for over a year. When planted in JI 2 it should be able to stay put for about three years without repotting, perhaps even longer with an annual top dressing. This takes only a few minutes and entails scraping away the top couple of inches of compost and replacing it with fresh. An old dessert spoon is a useful tool for this, and it won't matter if you destroy a few roots in the process. Any that are broken or badly damaged should be cut off cleanly and removed.

The avocado will probably need a stout bamboo cane to support it during its early months, but if grown in a good light, preferably close to a sunny window, it should soon become sturdy enough to do without ugly artificial supports.

THE DATE PALM

Although not as ornamental as some other palms, this is a quite prestigious object to have around when you can point to it as genuinely home-grown.

Planting

The date stone is something of a problem. It is very, very hard, sometimes infertile, and needs a lot of warmth to start it on its way. However, the date palm was first grown in this country in 1597, and it should find the average modern house an improvement on the best it could be offered then.

The only way of coping with the infertility problem is to plant as many stones as you can collect, but obviously you cannot have scores of pots cluttering the house all winter with no visible reason for their presence. Avoid wasting space, energy and compost by proceeding as follows:

Collect all the stones from your first box of dates and soak them in tepid water for forty eight hours like the avocado stone. Put a thick layer of well-moistened peat or soil-less compost in the bottom of a polythene bag, spread the date stones over it and cover them with another layer of peat or compost. Tie the top of the bag tightly to retain the moisture and place it in an airing cupboard or some other

Seedling date palms in Jiffy 7s.

really warm spot. When you accumulate another batch of stones, treat them in the same way, adding them to the same bag with enough additional compost to cover them. This can be repeated for as long as you go on eating dates or until enough stones have germinated. It is very little trouble, the contents of the bag needing only an occasional sprinkle of water and an inspection of the stones for signs of germination. Don't worry if they become mixed up at varying depths in the compost, all that matters is that they should be covered by it and kept warm and moist.

A stone that shows signs of germination – usually the appearance of a root – is potted up by itself in soil-less compost in a smallish pot. The stone should be about an inch below the surface and care must be taken not to break the root. The compost must be kept moist, and with the emergence of the shoot the pot must stand in a light place. A heated propagator is of course ideal, but a window sill in a warm room, especially if near a radiator, is good enough.

Continue to pot up hopeful-looking stones until you have as many as you want or it is obvious, after about two months, that no more will germinate. The plastic bag business is of course a familiar technique among gardeners for starting begonia and gloxinia tubers into growth.

General Management

The date palm is slow-growing under average room conditions and like all palms should not be over-potted. It can remain in soil-less compost and planted in JP 2, when it will hardly need feeding at all for the first couple of years. Water it freely in summer, but very sparingly in winter or whenever the temperature falls below 60°F (16°C).

A group of these little palms in a large planter or container – a sort of mini-oasis – is much more effective decoratively than a single specimen. But however arranged, keep them warm and out of draughts.

PEANUTS

Perhaps they are groundnuts or monkey nuts to you, but anyway they definitely are *not* nuts. Nor are they throwaways, for only perfectly sound ones are worth planting. They just happen to be so interesting that it's worth keeping a few for planting when next you are putting out the birds' winter rations.

The peanut is a leguminous plant, related, as its name implies, to the pea. It is an annual, and has developed the useful habit of planting its own seeds (the so-called nuts) by pushing them into the ground. Hence also 'groundnut', though I'm not sure where the monkeys came in. It was once widely grown in greenhouses as a curiosity.

A good deal of warmth is needed for germination, and a warm, sunny window for the peanut to complete its interesting life-cycle. It begins by looking like an overgrown clover, produces yellow, pea-like flowers in summer, followed by seed pods on downward-growing stems. These pods are pushed below the surface of the soil, and there they develop into the familiar nuts.

Planting and Management

Either shelled nuts or those still in the shell may be planted. If shelled ones are used make sure that they are not the roasted variety, and are not damaged. As a rule, better germination is to be expected from those still in their shells. They can be shelled and the seeds sown separately or the entire nut may be planted after being cracked across the middle to let the moisture in.

Peanuts should be planted in groups in fairly large pots. A 5″ half-pot is the minimum satisfactory size, and in this a number of peanuts can be planted close together near the centre and subsequently thinned to three or four seedlings if too many germinate. Use soil-less compost, either seed or potting, and plant an inch deep.

March and April are the best months to make a start, for the peanut must have summer light and warmth if it is to bloom and produce its strange seed pods. The seed needs a germinating temperature of not less than 70°F (21°C) and if it can be slightly higher, so much the better. A heated propagator gives the quickest results, but an unheated one, or a polythene-covered box, on a storage heater shelf will do the trick. But this sort of warmth for two or three weeks is absolutely essential if the peanuts are to sprout.

Once sprouted, keep them as warm as possible and in full light. As the plants grow, the compost, which should have been kept uniformly moist, will begin to dry out more quickly and you will have to give water more often. The plants must not be allowed to suffer from lack of water at any time, though they will need rather less after flowering. This period, when the long-stalked pods begin to form, is the most interesting in the peanut's career. At your first attempt you may not succeed in getting the plants to produce the ripe underground nuts, but this should not be impossible under ordinary room conditions. In hot weather the peanut plants will be better standing outdoors – but don't forget the regular and frequent watering.

No feeding is necessary, in fact they are better without any.

3 The Citrus Family

This is one of the greatest clans of edible fruits, its various members being grown in many parts of the world and the products consumed literally everywhere. This represents an awful lot of pips, and it seems a thousand pities that a few more of them are not allowed to grow into the glossy-leaved trees with the sweet-scented white flowers typical of the citrus species. And even, for this is well within the bounds of possibility, some real live fruit.

The different citrus species are very much inter-related and mixed up, so that they have certain basically similar characteristics. We can therefore describe the sowing of the pips and the treatment of the plants in a general way, covering all the familiar fruit, and then have a look at the individual species to see where any of them differ from the norm.

PIPS AND PIPLETS

The first thing to appreciate is that some citrus pips have strange habits. There is a factor common to most seeds of fruit trees to which this book often has to draw attention, and that is that trees grown from them will not be a reproduction of the parent tree. An apple tree from a Golden Delicious pip will not bear Golden Delicious Apples; the odds are that it will one day carry a sort of Mark Two Crab Apple. The seeds of a Black Hamburg grape may generate some fine vigorous vines, but it's odds on that their fruit will be small, skinny and acid. Some species, especially the peach, have a better chance of producing trees with usable fruit, and if you are prepared to rear thousands of seedlings you will eventually come up with something good – that is the only way in which new varieties can come into being. We cannot go into the reasons for this inability of fruit trees to 'breed true', suffice it that the genes in the fertilised germ cell get re-shuffled and the result is usually worse than better. So fruit trees have to be propagated vegetatively by grafting, budding or cuttings, and then each young one is exactly the same as its single parent.

The seed of citrus trees behaves in just the same way, producing offspring whose fruiting qualities are quite unpredictable, but it sometimes does something else which is very unusual. It produces more than one seedling from one seed.

This happens frequently with the lime, and fairly often with some varieties of orange. Growers of orange pips are apt to be puzzled when two or three seedlings appear in a little clump where only a solitary pip was planted. A seed which can thus sprout twins or triplets is described as being polyembryonic, and the family is far from normal. Only one of the group is a true seedling and has come from the fertilised germ cell in the pip. The other one, or two, as the case may be, originate from a quite different layer of cells and not from the fertilised germ. These extra seedlings are really being produced vegatively, like cuttings, and will grow into trees like that from which the pip came and bearing similar and equally good fruit. The one true seedling, though just as likely to make a pretty tree or shrub, may never have any fruit worth eating. It is rather as though a set of human triplets has one member with only incidental resemblances to either parent, while the other two are exact replicas of their mother.

The practical application of this for the pip-grower who aspires to a fruiting citrus tree is obvious. If several seedlings come up where you planted but one pip, cherish them all. Separate them carefully, pot them up, and try to keep them until they fruit in a few years time. Until that happens there is no way of identifying the sheep and goats. You may think it not worth waiting to find out, but remember that the young tree will be a worthy decoration for room, balcony, or patio, and that if they *do* fruit will be quite valuable. A fruiting orange tree will cost up to £5 now, and Heaven knows how much more by the time your piplets mature.

Planting

It's hardly necessary to say that only pips from ripe fruit should be planted, since you are not likely to be eating it unripe. Germination may be at its best in pips from fruit that is dead ripe to the point of squashiness, but it is not going to be at all good in those from the orange or lemon which has got mislaid and dried up to a shrivelled shell.

It is better to sow the pips fresh rather than dried, and the best time is early spring. Pips will germinate at any time of year given adequate warmth, but spring seedlings have the long, light days of summer before them in which to get established. The supply of some citrus fruit tends to be seasonal, and their pips must be sown when they become available. The tangerine is one of them, and usually appears at Christmas. It is well worth growing, forming a pretty, manageable pot plant which matures early and often bears edible fruit.

A makeshift propagator:
Orange seedling in jam jar.

The planting of the pips can be done in a variety of ways in any seed compost and a temperature of 60°-70°F (16°-21°C). Some sort of propagator is a help, even a makeshift one. For instance you can put some drainage crocks at the bottom of a jam jar, add a couple of inches of soil-less compost, push two or three pips just below the surface, and water gently. Then close the jar with a square of polythene and an elastic band and stand it by a radiator or on the mantelpiece. As soon as a pip germinates and the seed-leaves are fully expanded fish it out carefully with a table fork and pot it up in a small peat pot.

My own preference is for planting the pips individually in peat pots or Jiffy 7s and putting a small trayful of these in a propagator or a polythene bag. Individually grown plants are easier to handle and better in every way. Of course, you will be left with a number of blank pots, but these can be used for a future batch of plantings.

One generally sows several seeds in a small peat pot and reduces the seedlings to one, but with citrus seed you could never be sure whether several pips had germinated or whether you had got a family group from a single polyembryonic pip. In the latter

Ten-week-old orange in square peat pot.

case you would want to preserve all the seedlings in the hope of one day picking fruit, and if several seedlings appear in a pot you know to contain only one pip these will be the potentially valuable ones. For the same reason, if a number of seeds are sown in a larger pot, they should be spaced about one and a half inches apart so that any multiple sproutings occurring will be easily spotted. Label your pips at planting time; different citrus species look much alike in their young days and as they grow up it helps to know which members of the family you are dealing with.

Pips should not be sown more than half an inch deep, they prefer shallow planting and if deeply buried the seed-leaves may be distorted on emergence. Being near the surface entails care in seeing that they don't dry out; even closed in a polythene bag it is wise to check the compost for moisture every three or four days. Use slightly warm water for both pips and piplets.

It is quite possible to get results by planting the

pips at any time in the pots of other house plants, as already suggested. If this is done in the winter they must be fostered on a plant such as a maranta, which is kept warm and moist. If you grow saintpaulias and resort to the old humidifying trick of keeping the saintpaulia pots in bowls of moist peat you can try some citrus pips in the peat. Temperature and conditions that suit the saintpaulia would be good enough to start an orange pip. Like many such things in gardening, this method of popping something in and practically forgetting it often works surprisingly well. But you must transfer the seedlings from their foster homes to pots of their own at the first opportunity.

Germinating time for most citrus seeds is three to four weeks on average, which in practice means anything from a fortnight to a couple of months.

Later Management

After a full season's growth your citrus plant will be three to five inches high, according to species and conditions. Growth is steady in summer and may continue slowly in winter if the temperature is around the ordinary central heating level. On the whole a lower winter temperature is probably better, for the citrus family seems to flourish in areas having a marked difference between summer and winter, though without severe cold. Hence its very early spread in the Mediterranean lands. It also, at least for most species, likes a contrast between day and night temperatures and not a steady hothouse or 'tropical' warmth.

We shall find that some citrus fruit trees can even stand a certain amount of frost, but as a general rule it is safer to winter any citrus in a room where the thermometer won't fall much below 40°F (6°C). The important point is that these are not soft-leaved exotics, but tough evergreens, revelling in sun and air and natural warmth, and happy to stand out-doors, even in an English summer.

The young plant is of course more tender than the mature tree, and should be kept out of cold draughts for the first few months. It needs full sun in a south or west facing window. The only exception to this is after repotting, when it should stand in the shade for a few days. When it becomes a fair-sized shrub it will tolerate less light for limited periods, which is lucky because you can't have a six-foot tree per-manently in the window. When it reaches this size you have several alternatives: you can give it a window to itself in a spare bedroom or some such place; you can keep it in a convenient spot for carry-ing outdoors on good summer days – it's a pity to leave it out permanently when in bloom because one then misses so much of the fragrance and beauty of the flowers – or you can see that it has a few hours daily of bright artificial light. All the citruses respond to artificial lighting if they are close to the light source. Incandescent bulbs may scorch the leaves and fluorescent tubes are better. Best of all are the special tubes such as 'Grolux', designed for indoor gardening.

Having said all that it remains true that hundreds of people keep healthy orange, lemon and grapefruit trees in their living rooms for years and years with-out, as they say, taking a bit of trouble.

Composts and Potting

Citrus trees grow in most soils provided they are well-drained and can be given plenty of water with-out becoming waterlogged. When planted in con-tainers they repay generous treatment, giving best results in a good compost and with a certain amount of feeding.

For the first two years a soil-less compost is suitable, with fortnightly liquid feeds in summer. Moves to successively larger pots will be needed, and when you get to the 6″ size JIP 3 compost should be used. With this compost annual repotting is avoided, a top dressing is given every year, the top two inches of compost being scraped away and replaced, and the tree repotted every two or three years.

Fruiting trees are going to need 12″ pots or small tubs – oranges have been grown in tubs in this country for centuries – but those kept purely for decoration will probably not need more than a 9″ pot. The citrus tree looks well in any sort of ceramic container, or in a good quality plastic type with a pseudo-ceramic or stoneware finish. Indoors it must stand in a large saucer or dish to take the drainage from the considerable amounts of water and liquid fertiliser used in the warm months of the year.

Watering is really determined by temperature and growth. The tree may need ten times as much when in full growth as when resting in the 'cold' months. At all times of the year it appreciates overhead sprinkling or spraying with tepid water to freshen the leaves and remove dust. Cleaning the leaves with a damp cloth now and then is worth the time spent, the charm of citrus trees depending a lot on their shining foliage. Yellowing leaves will appear on the older trees, but this is not a symptom of disease. Evergreens replace old leaves at any time of the year; yellow ones are simply being discarded and should be removed.

Now for a closer look at some of the citrus whose pips are most often planted, beginning with the best known of all.

THE ORANGE

It apparently came from the Far East and spread all over in a series of jumps. The Arabs brought it from India to the Eastern Mediterranean. The Islamic conquests started its cultivation in North Africa and Spain, the Crusaders brought it to Italy and Provence. Now its many varieties grow from Israel to California, from the Pyrenees to the Cape of Good Hope. It really is a very adaptable tree.

Countries like Britain had to rely on imports for their main supply of oranges and consumption of them here increased steadily. Sweet Nell was hawking them with remarkable effect about 1650, and by 1850 they were a serious preoccupation of the Metropolitan Police. Scotland Yard issued repeated directives:

'Complaint has been again made to the Commissioner of the danger to foot-passengers from orange-peel thrown on the footways. The attention of the whole of the Police is again directed to this subject ... Constables are to remove pieces of orange-peel whenever seen on the pavement.'

However, people in northern latitudes were not content with consuming oranges, wasting the pips and scattering the peel. They actually tried to grow them.

In 1526 Sir Francis Carew was planting orange trees in Surrey, protecting them in winter by enclosing them in wooden huts. It says much for the toughness of the species that these trees survived for two centuries, being killed by the fierce winter of 1739; whether they ever ripened fruit is another matter.

Samuel Pepys was in Hackney a few months before the Great Fire, and 'Here I first saw oranges grow, some green, some half, some quarter, some full ripe, on the same tree, and one fruit of the same tree do come a year or two after the other; I pulled off a little one by stealth (the man being mightily curious of them) and eat it, and it was just as other little green oranges are, as big as half the end of my little finger'. Pepys had noticed one peculiarity of the citrus family – the way in which successive crops of fruit overlap. An orange takes from nine to twelve months to grow and ripen, so that when the first flowers open in the spring the tree may still be carrying the previous year's crop. The speed of ripening is largely dependent on temperature, as is the quality and sweetness of the fruit. A mean summer and autumn temperature of 65°F (18°C) – difficult to attain in our climate – is needed to ripen the current year's crop by Christmas.

Orange-growing became a status symbol in Britain in the eighteenth century, and the early greenhouses and conservatories were usually called orangeries. Most of them were highly inefficient, poorly heated and with quite inadequate light. They were useful for the winter protection of citrus trees in tubs, but on the whole provided them with poorer conditions than they would get in a modern dwelling house. Despite this, ripe fruit was produced when management was good.

Species of Orange

From which sorts are the pips most worth planting? The Sweet Orange, Citrus *sinensis*, includes all the larger dessert varieties, the blood orange, the Jaffa, and so on. Trees from any of these will be rather large and slow-growing. They can be pruned by shortening long shoots at any time of the year, but may eventually need an 18″ pot or tub. When grown from pips they may not fruit for six to eight

years and unless you raise a group of seedlings from
a polyembryonic pip it's impossible to know in
advance if the fruit is going to be eatable. For decoration, the tree is very effective. It has few of the
sharp spines which some of the citruses carry, and
the single or clustered white flowers in the axile of
the pale green leaves are almost overwhelmingly
fragrant.

The Seville or Sour Orange. Citrus *aurantium*, is
of course the marmalade orange. No-one in this
country would want to grow it for its fruit, but it
has a few advantages for the pipster. It produces lots
of seeds and their germination is pretty good. In
fact many Seville seedlings are raised commercially
as rootstocks on which other varieties are grafted.
It blossoms freely and is one of the hardiest oranges,
surviving quite severe frosts.

The Mandarin Orange, Citrus *reticulata*, includes
the tinies of the family, tangerines, clementines and
satsumas. They are among the best for pot plants,
being relatively small, quick-maturing, and able to
fruit in 12″ pots. They are even more frost-resistant
than the Seville, but only because they become dormant as soon as the temperature falls below 60°F
(16°C). A fruiting tree of any of these varieties must
therefore be brought into a temperature of about
65°F (18°C) as early as possible in the spring to induce growth and flowering. In a continuously warm
climate the mandarins blossom more than once a
year, but under our conditions one must make the
most of the summer by getting them to bloom as
early as possible. The fruit must develop during the
warm months, for low temperatures make it almost
uneatably sour.

The tangerine is the best source of pips among the
mini-oranges. Many of its seeds are polyembryonic,

producing seedlings that will eventually bear good fruit. The satsuma is usually seedless, or nearly so, but try any satsuma pips you happen to find. The clementine is seedless when the blossom has not been fertilised, when it *does* have seeds they will not breed true and the fruit may be useless. But all these varieties are attractive shrubby plants with willowy branches (sometimes bowed to the ground by the weight of fruit) and the usual scented blossoms.

THE LEMON

Several varieties of lemon exist, though it is only a single species – Citrus *limonia*. Like the orange it probably came from the East and spread in the same haphazard way. It was soon established around the Mediterranean and was an early migrant to the New World, Columbus taking it to Haiti in 1493. Today the Mediterranean and California are its main areas of production.

Mention of California reminds one that the lemon grows easily from seed. Named varieties were scarcely known until the Americans started breeding and selecting, and one still in cultivation came from a pip sown in Los Angeles in 1858 and subsequently multiplied by budding and cuttings.

Lemon trees were probably first grown in England in the sixteenth century in tubs standing outdoors in the summer and being wintered inside. They never aroused as much interest as oranges, perhaps because of the less useful fruit, but the trees had the merits of hardiness and small size. A lemon tree may be in full bearing when only eight feet high and will have started to fruit long before reaching that height. Temperatures as low as 22°F (−6°C) are needed to kill the mature wood, though anything below freezing point will injure young shoots and fruit; it is wise to observe the general rule for all citrus trees and winter the lemon in a room kept above freezing. It starts growing in the spring as soon as the mercury climbs above 50°F (10°C) and will flower at intervals through the summer. The fruit formed then remains on the tree, undamaged unless actually frozen, and ripens the following summer. This overwintering of the immature fruit is supposed to improve it, making it more acid and generally lemony.

The lemon's toleration of low temperatures applies even to its pips. Only 55°F (13°C) is needed to germinate them, so they can be started on the window sill without artificial warmth practically any time from April to October. They will not breed true, for the lemon produces very few polyembryonic seeds, but few of us can distinguish one lemon from another. The seedlings grow quickly when started in individual pots and need little attention apart from regular watering.

Cuttings may be taken from the lemon tree in July, and this is a quick way of increasing your own stock or of acquiring young trees to give away. Stem cuttings from the current year, three to four inches long are inserted in a pot of sandy compost or singly in Jiffy 7s. They are kept warm and moist in a propagator or polythene bag and should form roots in a few weeks. Cuttings may also be taken from the previous year's growth if it is not too hard and woody.

A 12" pot of JIP 3 compost is large enough for a fruiting lemon if it is given regular liquid feeds in summer. It will need repotting in alternate years, and the best time for this operation is March, when the tree is about to start into growth. If the tree is to be replaced in the same sized pot some of the compost must be removed from the outside of the soil ball, but it should never be broken up so completely as to leave the whole root system exposed; this of course applies to all repotting. The repotted tree should be left in a shady position for a fortnight and the compost kept nicely moist. It should not be watered heavily or given liquid fertiliser until the disturbed roots have had time to make firm contact with the soil.

Pruning

Citrus trees do not on the whole respond to pruning like, say, apple trees. You can never be sure that if you cut back an unwanted branch another will grow in a more convenient position. It would be almost impossible to train a citrus of any sort in the form of an espalier.

It may sometimes be necessary to cut off the top of a tree which is shooting up like a bean pole and producing no laterals; this is not the sort of behaviour that can be tolerated in a domesticated plant with restricted living-space, it must be decapitated and compelled to branch out *somewhere* if not exactly where you want it to.

This is unlikely to be necessary with the lemon. It doesn't grow tall and it is a naturally spreading tree with plenty of small branches. Almost an ideal shape for decoration, especially as the young leaves and shoots are of a reddish tint against the pale shining green of the adult foliage. The flower buds are similarly tinted, though the big star-shaped flowers are pure white.

The lemon has one pruning problem, however, which occurs in most citrus species, though not to the same extent. A tree approaching maturity – that is, beginning to blossom – may start producing a

*Orange tree with the
leader cut back to induce
bushier growth. Citrus
trees need very little
pruning but must not be
allowed to grow too tall.*

number of fast-growing, unwanted shoots in the
wrong places. These growths, known as 'water
sprouts', spring from the upper sides of young lateral branches and grow straight up, parallel with the
main stem. They are rampant, sappy things, growing
much faster than the branches from which they
originate and sometimes crowding the centre of the
tree and making it too tall. They should be cut out
completely, though where they spring from near the
tip of a branch and are well clear of the main stem
they can be shortened and allowed to remain. In this
position they eventually sober down and produce
flowers and fruit.

Look out for your hands when pruning lemons –
they have sharp little spines in the most unexpected
places.

THE GRAPEFRUIT

The ancestry of the grapefruit is something that not
even the College of Heralds cound unravel. It started
in Asia or the South Seas as the pummelo, bearing
the largest flowers and fruit of any citrus. A Captain
Shaddock took it to the West Indies, where from
being large it became enormous and was named the
shaddock. Shaddocks are said to have reached
weights of fourteen pounds apiece, though their
quality suffered. In the eighteenth century an improved pummelo/shaddock appeared, smaller but
nicer, and by 1840 the Jamaicans were calling it a
grapefruit. So the grapefruit may have come from
the shaddock, which came from the pummelo, or
they may, as some botanists swear, have been separate species from the beginning. I don't want to start
another argument, but where did the pink-fleshed
ugli, which once seemed to be catching on here,
come from . . . ?

Grapefruit pips need the same treatment as those
of the orange. Germination is pretty good but there
are no polyembryonic seeds, so what sort of fruit
you may one day pick is a toss-up. Seedless grapefruit are abundant nowadays, but even they will
probably provide you with enough pips to plant.
The commercial definition of seedless is 'having six
pips or less'.

Growth of the tree is quite rapid as it is naturally
tall. It also branches freely and makes denser foliage
than most of the citrus family. You will do no harm
by stopping the main leader when you think it is
high enough.

Grapefruit trees have the annoying habit of producing a few blooms while still quite small and then
no more for a year or two. The blossoms are not as

well placed as in other members of the family, being borne on the tips of shoots instead of nestling among the leaves. But they make up for this by their impressive size and strong perfume.

THE LIME

This anti-scorbutic fruit which became part of the Royal Navy's diet, and so provided the Americans with a nickname for the British in general, is seldom enjoyed here as fresh fruit. It is available though, and its pips are worth planting.

It came, of course, from the East. It was brought to the Levant by the Arabs, and to other places by the Crusaders and to the Americas by . . . yes, you've guessed it. I sometimes feel that Saladin and King Richard and Columbus must have spent most of their time transporting citrus trees.

The lime produces mainly polyembryonic seed, and so trees raised from pips almost invariably carry usable fruit. The pips require the same treatment as those of the orange, but the seedlings are somewhat slower in growth. The mature tree is bushy and spreading; it is definitely more tender than the lemon, but is perfectly safe in a winter temperature of 40°F (6°C) or above.

The flowers are rather small, but appear almost continuously under warm conditions. The tree can stand outdoors from May to September.

The ripe fruit is small, of a distinctive greenish yellow colour, and with a unique scent. The high vitamin content of the juice is well known. Less well known is the fact that when applied to the skin it helps to promote a good sun tan.

4 Plants from the Kitchen

A number of things found in the average shopping basket, or consigned to the kitchen waste-bin, could be made to grow into plants. When it comes to growing things, though, it's better not to develop an uncritical enthusiasm. Plants must not be reared and given precious house-room purely as a demonstration of horticultural skill; they must have some intrinsic value, be nice to look at or in some way curious and amusing.

Two of the subjects suggested in this chapter, the pineapple and the coffee tree, score on all counts. They are quite a test of indoor gardening, they are unusual, and above all they are as decorative as anything the florist can offer.

CARROT TOPS

A King of Siam is supposed to have cultivated carrots for the beauty of their foliage. It seems an unlikely story from a land renowned for its tropical flora, but no doubt Thailand, like ourselves, has had some peculiar monarchs. Even in this country carrot leaves have a long ornamental tradition. Parkinson, writing in the seventeenth century, says 'The leaves in Autumn turn to be of a fine red or purple, the beauty whereof allureth many Gentlewomen oftentimes to gather the leaves and stick them in their hats or heads, or pin them on their arms in stead of feathers'. All of which sounds depressingly painful.

The indoor growing of carrot foliage has hitherto been left mainly to the children, but the flower arrangers and others have come to appreciate the value of the light feathery foliage in the winter months.

Preparation and Planting

When preparing carrots for cooking, save the tops of large, healthy-looking specimens which have been trimmed so as to leave the 'crown' – the remnant of buds where the tuft of leaves has been cut. If the whole top has been sliced off already, leaving a surface of bare flesh, there will be nothing left to grow and the carrot is only for cooking. If the top seems reasonably intact, cut it off with about an inch of the root and plant it straightaway. The larger the carrot the more impressive will be the resultant bunch of foliage. Only the maincrop carrots, bought in winter, can be used, the small bunched varieties sold in summer are useless, and anyway, who wants carrot foliage in summer? Washed and pre-packed carrots will probably grow if the crown of the root is still there, but you will not, I hope, expect results from frozen ones.

Plant your carrot tops in soil-less compost, at such a depth that they are just flush with the surface, neither covered nor protruding. The entire piece of carrot should be underground where it will develop roots, so feeding the growing top and holding it steady.

One is still sometimes advised to grow carrot tops in saucers of water or containers of wet pebbles, but the method is ugly, messy, and apart from amusing the kids, has nothing to commend it. On the other hand, a group of five or six tops, planted in a 5″ half-pot, produces a genuinely decorative cluster of fern.

This 'fern' is also useful where a foliage backing

for spring flowering bulbs in containers is required. You can plant the carrot tops directly among the bulbs when the latter are first brought in from the plunge bed or dark cupboard, but if they grow badly or unevenly you risk spoiling the whole appearance of the bulb bowl. A better way is to grow the carrots separately in peat pots, planting them among the bulbs when the foliage is well advanced. Use the smallest size of peat pot into which the top will fit. and plant about three weeks before the bulbs are expected to flower. If you have already decided to try this at bulb-planting time leave enough space between the bulbs to insert the carrot tops without serious disturbance. If this arrangement succeeds the effect is at least as good as the nurseryman obtains with his unrooted sprigs of ivy and tradescantia.

One last carrot trick has no great aesthetic value but always attracts attention if it works. You need the largest carrot you can find, and I'm afraid you are going to waste half of it. Cut off the top with about three inches of root and remove the core of this bit of root, leaving it hollow but with fairly thick sides. Make three equidistant holes in the sides and thread enough string through them to hang the thing head downwards. Then fill the cavity with water and keep it filled. If all goes well the fern will sprout from the bottom and continue to grow; if not, the carrot will speedily go rotten. In any case it should, like all suspended vegetation, be hung well clear of everyones' heads. Nobody wants an eyeful of cold tincture of carrot.

BEETROOT AND PARSNIP

These can be treated in the same way as carrots, though a considerable thickness of root must be left on the beet top. It would also have a better chance if from one of the new non-bleeding varieties. If you have any beet which appear too small and withered to be of any culinary use you should plant the entire root. This is pretty sure to result in a nice batch of purple-veined tinted leaves which flower arrangers seem happy to use all the year round. A sunny window sill is the right place to ensure full colouration of the beet leaves.

There appears to be no reason why the tops of swedes and turnips should not be sprouted in the same way, but one has to draw the line somewhere. All these vegetable roots require only a very moderate temperature to start them into growth, and will last much longer in a relatively cool room. It should be remembered that you are only taking advantage of a natural process; these biennial vegetables store up foodstuffs in their roots to give themselves a rapid start in spring. You are merely inducing them to do it in midwinter – while using most of the stored-up nutrients yourself.

THE PINEAPPLE'S POLL

The pineapple has, or should have, a little topknot of leaves. This is cut off when you serve the fruit, but should not be thrown away because it's the basis of a new pineapple plant. I said that the pineapple should still have its topknot, because there are reports that some being offered for sale have been scalped. The suggestion is that the tops are being removed and sold to nurserymen, who now realise that this is a valuable house plant. Propagation of the pineapple is normally by suckers growing from the base of the plant, though when there is a shortage of this material the alternative method of rooting the top tuft of leaves has always been employed.

Pineapples belong to the bromeliad family, many of which are popular indoor plants, especially in the United States where they enjoy the customary high room temperatures. Pineapple plants are larger than most of the cultivated bromeliads, the graceful tapering leaves covering a 3' spread under good conditions. In the midst of this arching foliage a thick stem arises, bearing a cluster of purplish flowers and ultimately a single fruit.

Whether the plant can be fruited under room conditions I don't know; it can certainly be grown successfully as an ornamental species, and it can be fairly easily fruited in the greenhouse. Magnificent fruit were being grown in English hothouses 150 years ago, some of them weighing 5 lbs. apiece. But they were costly to grow and their cultivation was allowed to lapse when high quality imports became available. The advent of canning later transformed the fruit from a luxury into a commonplace.

Planting

Cut off the top of the pineapple with a disc of flesh about half an inch thick. Leave this portion for forty-eight hours with the cut surface uppermost to dry out. Just before planting it may be slightly moistened again and sprinkled with hormone rooting powder, but this is not essential.

What *is* essential is the use of a really well-drained compost, and the very best is a soil-less seed and cutting compost to which a small quantity of coarse sand has been added. The size of pot used is determined by the diameter of the sliced-off top; this must be accommodated with at least an inch to spare all round to facilitate watering. The pot need

Another make-shift propagator. This pineapple top is being rooted in a polythene bag kept in warmth and light.

not be very deep but good drainage is so vital that a layer of crocks or pebbles should be placed at the bottom of it.

The pineapple top is planted with the slice of flesh just covered but not buried deeply. The little tuft of leaves should be well clear of the compost. After planting, water the pot gently and stand it in a warm place. Water used should be tepid, as for the avocado, and if possible this should be so throughout the pineapple's life.

To get the topknot to root and grow into a new plant, plenty of warmth is essential. Bottom heat is always a help in the quick rooting of cuttings and this is merely an unusual form of cutting. Failure to

induce rooting is more often due to a low temperature than to anything else. A heated propagator or
the glass or polythene-covered box over the storage
heater gives the right sort of heat, and if a thermometer registers anything between 70°F and 80°F
(21° and 27°C) when placed near the pot you can be
reasonably sure that the pineapple will grow. It is
much less likely to do so on a living room window
sill where the temperature is in the sixties by day
and appreciably lower at night.

General Management

The first sign that the pineapple top is rooting will
be the appearance of new leaves in the centre of the
crown and renewed growth of the existing ones.
Keep it in its warm spot, shut in and protected from
draughts but getting as much light as possible, until
this growth is really obvious. Then move the plant
to its permanent home in the warmest and lightest
spot you can find.

If there seems to be a good deal of emphasis on
warmth it is because this is so important. The pineapple, once established, will put up with quite a lot
of neglect. It won't mind if you forget to water it
for days on end, for instance, and it will tolerate
living in an absurdly small pot. Although it benefits
from regular feeding the only effect of starving it is
that the foliage is less spectacular. But it cannot
stand being cold, and temperatures of a few degrees
above freezing point can do it lasting damage. It
most appreciates a winter temperature of 65°F
(18°C) and a summer one rising to 90°F (32°C). As
a general and practicable rule we could say keep it
between 60° and 80°F (16° and 27°C) which in a
normal year in the average house is not difficult.

Like most bromeliads, the pineapple has a small

root system and does not need a deep container. A well-grown plant does, however, need a fairly wide one if it is to stand firmly, such as a large half-pot or a bowl-shaped decorative container with a drainage hole. A soil-less potting compost is suitable and with fortnightly liquid feeds in the summer the pineapple will only need repotting in alternate years. This is best done in late spring or early summer.

I have said that the pineapple will tolerate drought and semi-starvation, but generous watering and feeding in the growing season (May-September) produces longer and more striking foliage. The early English growers soon came to realise this, finding that the more leaf a plant carried the larger and more luscious was the ultimate fruit.

If provided with really good conditions, the pineapple will begin to push up its central flowering stem during its second year, though it will need a good deal of luck and experience to produce an actual fruit under ordinary room conditions. If it has shown no sign of flowering by the end of the second year, try enclosing it in a large plastic bag with several apples for a week. The apples give off the gas ethylene which stimulates the formation of flower buds in the pineapple.

THE COFFEE TREE

Which is what it is, strictly speaking, though grown more as a bush commercially and as a pretty evergreen pot plant indoors.

In America the coffee tree is a valued pot plant and the beans can be bought from seedsmen by the enterprising indoor gardener. Indeed, it is advertised as a pot plant that will produce flowers and fruit while still of a manageable size. Here, the seedsmen have so far ignored it, so we must take our chance with a few *unroasted* beans – which can usually be cadged from any grocer who roasts and grinds his own coffee.

Coffee came from Africa, possibly from the Ethiopean province of Kaffia. The Arabs began using the bean in the fifteenth century and when its use spread to Europe it was planted commercially in many countries. Although it will not grow outdoors in temperate climates the tree is tougher than many tropical introductions. It will grow at high altitudes and there produce the highest quality coffee, indicating that a relatively cool period suits it.

Planting

Although the adult tree does not need consistently high temperatures the bean definitely needs one to start it into growth. We are once more faced with a tropical seed that must have tropical warmth for those initial weeks.

The coffee bean in fact must be given exactly the same treatment as the pineapple top, and the nearer to 80°F (27°C) you can keep it the sooner it will germinate. The seeds – they are not true beans – are sown about half an inch deep in soil-less compost in small pots, or in Jiffy 7s. In a heated propagator or similar well-warmed spot, germination will take about three weeks. If several beans have been sown in each pot, they should be reduced to single seedlings and kept in the propagator until they are a few inches high. Then they can be transferred to a warm, sunny window sill.

March and April are the best months for starting the coffee beans, as the seedlings will make nice little plants by the end of the summer. If you think of using natural rather than artificial warmth to assist in germination, however, sow them in July, placing the pots on a south-facing window sill, in any type of unheated propagator, or simply covered with polythene and brown paper or cardboard. Keep the compost always moist, preferably using tepid water.

General Management

The seedlings can remain in small pots through their first winter, during which time they should be kept only just moist. In the spring, repot them into 5″ pots of soil-less or JIP 2 compost. The latter is really best, as you can forget about any further re-potting for at least two years.

A winter temperature around 60°F (16°C) and a summer one of 65°-75°F (18°-23°C) is adequate for the coffee tree once past its seedling stage. Water it freely in summer, giving an occasional liquid feed, but only sparingly during the cooler months. Good drainage is very important, and the pot should have a layer of crocks or pebbles at the bottom.

Its dark green, glossy leaves are sufficient reason for having a coffee tree in the home, but by the third year you may begin to get the extra bonus of flowers. These are borne in clusters among the leaves, fragrant, pure white and strikingly beautiful. Unfortunately, they are short-lived, but the same plant may bloom more than once in the year. The fruit is a large green berry, changing to a bright red when ripe and containing two 'beans'.

Having reared one coffee tree you raise more from cuttings. These are taken in summer and will root with the ordinary treatment described in Chapter 1. Be careful from what part of the tree you take them, though, for it has some unusual growth habits. There may be one central stem, or more than one. From the vertical stem grow lateral branches in pairs, one from each side of the main stem, exactly opposite and perfectly horizontal. Other laterals will eventually grow from these, still horizontal, turning neither up nor down. If you take cuttings from any of these laterals they will root alright, but they won't grow *up* – they will continue to grow horizontally along the ground, in the same position as when attached to the parent stem. To produce a normal plant you must take the top two or three inches of a main stem, cut just below a pair of leaves and the bottom leaves stripped off. Use either vermiculite or a mixture of soil-less compost and coarse sand as the rooting medium, and keep warm and close in a polythene bag or a propagator.

THE SWEET POTATO

This, of course, is the one that Ol' Man River didn't plant. I believe that many of those consumed here come from the Southern United States. It is slowly gaining in popularity here, and is hardy enough to be grown outdoors.

The frantically active twining tops, which may outgrow the runner bean given a support to cling to, don't conform to our ideas of conventional potato behaviour. The thing is really an Ipomoea and related to the lovely Morning Glory. Its flowers are relatively colourless but are sweetly scented.

The real reason for diverting a couple of tubers from the shopping basket to the indoor garden is its turn of speed as a climber. There are many types of decorative foliage and flowering plants to be grown from the unconsidered trifles of an average house-

hold, but few climbers are among them. Various
beans may be attempted, and so may ordinary potatoes, which become so long and straggly as to merit
the description of climbers whilst looking most un-
lovely. Moreover, they get infested with aphids,
which spread to other plants.

The sweet potato, however, is a natural climber
and in a warm, light room will make its way up any
form of support and be, as they say, 'well furnished'
with leaves. It may even flower.

Planting

The question of which way up to plant sweet potatoes arouses a lot of argument. They are variable in
shape, without the well-defined 'rose' end in which
the dormant buds or eyes are clustered, as in the
ordinary potato. It is sometimes suggested that they
should be started in wet moss, or even in water like
an avocado pit, and finally planted only when the
roots and shoots have plainly declared themselves.

This is quite unnecessary. Whichever way you
plant the tuber roots always go down and shoots
come up, even if they perform a somersault to do it.
The important thing is not to make things more difficult for the shoot by having it buried too deeply.

Choose a pot of medium size, about 6", and fill it
two-thirds full with soil-less potting compost. Dam-
pen this thoroughly and lay two or three tubers on
it. Cover them with an inch of compost and place
the pot in a temperature as near 65°F (18°C) as you
can manage. There is no specific planting time, and
I understand that sweet potatoes are now available
all the year round. If your retailer can assure you
that the tubers have not been artificially dried there
is no reason why they should not soon start into
growth.

When the shoots emerge, reduce them to only two to each tuber and keep them in a sunny position. Add more compost as the vines grow until the pot is filled to within an inch of the top, and keep well watered at all times.

5 Hardy Trees

So far we have considered only trees which could not survive outdoors in our climate, grown from the seeds of imported fruit. But the seeds and pips of our own forest trees and fruit trees are as readily come by and easy to grow. Many of them make charming house plants up to the two-year-old stage and can be used in miniature gardens. Some species, notably the oak, beech, apple, sycamore and hawthorn, are good basic material for *bonsai*, and if you intend to practise this fascinating art a few home-grown deciduous seedlings will be as suitable for your first attempts as expensive bought conifers.

Fruit tree seeds, apple, pear, plum and peach, are going to be available at various times in the year, but for reasons to be explained in a moment autumn and winter are the best times to make a start with them. The seeds of forest and hedgerow trees, which can be gathered on country walks or in parks and gardens, are only ready in autumn — when the 'conkers' begin to fall.

Planting

The germination of these seeds and fruits (the acorn, the conker, and the winged 'keys' of ash and sycamore are really fruits) can be a slow business. Indeed, if they are popped straight into pots of compost in a warm room they may resolutely refuse to do anything and ultimately get themselves slung out in disgust. To avoid this sort of disappointment one should look at what happens to tree seeds in nature, because if a presumably fertile seed fails to germinate when provided with the essentials of warmth and moisture there must be something else wrong with its environment.

Consider, then, an acorn which has fallen from the tree and escaped being eaten. Perhaps it has rolled into a shallow crack in the ground with a few rotting leaves over it. There it will lie for the whole winter, soaked with rain, covered with snow, frozen for days on end in iron-hard soil. Its tough outer casing is softened and the embryo inside is ready to start growing when soil temperatures rise in spring. Or take the seed of an ash tree, whirling down on its translucent wings which slowly decay and are dragged into the soil by earthworms. You will see no sign of seedlings until the following summer, but then, if the tree is near your garden, you will find baby ash trees appearing even from rose beds and crazy paving.

The thing to remember is that all seeds need a period of dormancy before they are ready to germinate. In some this period is very short, but among trees it may be much longer. In temperate climates the dormant period is passed with the seed exposed to the rigours of winter, and when we attempt to short-cut this part of the cycle the seed either refuses to function or is terribly slow about it. The preliminary treatment needed to get round the problem may seem a waste of time, but it has long been used in the germination of tree seeds.

Stratification. This simply means exposing your collected pips and stones to wet and wintry weather for a couple of months before planting them in warmth. Store them in a cool place until about Christmas, then turn them outdoors.

You can plant them in pots of compost, covering the seed only lightly, and then stand them in a completely unsheltered position. Bring them in to a temperature of 55-60°F (13-16°C) at the beginning of March. Plant several stones or pips of a species in each pot, and as they germinate one at a time over a period of weeks move them immediately to small individual pots.

Another, and I think a better way, of exposing the seeds is to put them in tins of damp sand. The trouble with using pots is that the pips are a standing temptation to birds and field mice and you are always likely to find the whole lot scratched up or just neatly excavated and eaten. And, if earthenware pots are used, they may split if the contents freeze solid.

Any type of tin will do provided it has a lid to keep out robbers. Punch a few holes in the bottom for drainage and a few in the lid for air. Put in a layer of damp sand, spread your pips, seeds, hawthorn berries, acorns, chestnuts, or what-have-you over it, and cover them with another layer of damp sand. This covering layer must be only deep enough just to hide the largest seeds; they are living things – even if they don't look it – and must have oxygen. You could, of course, use peat instead of sand, but when you come to disinter them you will find the smaller pips easier to locate against the light background of sand than if they were mixed up in dark brown peat.

The actual planting can be in ordinary small pots or in Jiffy pots. The smaller seeds could go into Jiffy 7s, but the larger ones would need a 3" pot. Or, as already suggested, they can be planted in batches in larger containers and transplanted promptly on germination. The early move to an individual pot is advisable because so many tree species put down a large and easily damaged tap root very quickly and will suffer less of a check if you can move them with this intact.

Soil-less potting compost is a good growing medium. Trees do well in it while small, and when they cease to be small you will have to part with them and raise a new generation. Ordinary room temperatures are quite high enough for germination, but if you can stand the pots of seeds in an unheated propagator or cover them with polythene, you will have less watering to do. *They must never be allowed to dry out or your efforts will be wasted.* Depth of planting, time taken to germinate, and other details, are mentioned when we come to individual varieties.

Finally, on this business of germinating seeds, it may for various reasons be impossible for you to treat them to a prolonged course of cold and damp. You can still get reasonable results in many cases if you remember to:

Always save fruit stones and pips from fully ripe fruit. Plum stones should come away cleanly from the flesh and apple pips be dark brown or black in colour. A Cox's Orange Pippin, of course, is ripe when the pips rattle inside it. Apples which have been kept through the winter and become withered with age will provide the liveliest pips.

Soak hard stones and pips in tepid water for forty-eight hours before planting.

Crack the hard shells of plum and peach stones. This is a substitute for the slow natural process of stratification. It needs to be done carefully, the shell being squeezed gently in a pair of nutcrackers until it begins to fracture.

Delay sowing until late winter or early spring, storing the pips in the coolest place you can find.

General Management

All these trees are deciduous, which means that their leaves will fall in the autumn and they will rest until spring. Their decorative value in winter is practically nil and during this time they should be banished to a really cool room and given only enough water to keep the compost moist.

In February, when the days are lengthening, they can be brought into a warm living room and given a well-lit window sill; then you will have the pleasure of seeing the fresh bright green of spring unfolding early. This will happen one year after planting the pips, though the trees will still be very small. By the second spring they will be much larger and very decorative subjects for early summer, especially the chestnut with its big palmate leaves.

One exception to the general behaviour is the oak. Although a normally deciduous tree in the open it often keeps its leaves all the year round when grown indoors. I remember a tiny oak tree in a miniature garden which remained green throughout the winter.

The trees will need plenty of water in the summer, but feeding is usually inadvisable – the slower they grow the longer you can keep them indoors. For the same reason the final potting should be to a 5″ pot or thereabouts; when a tree gets too large for this size it will probably have outgrown its welcome and can be given away or planted outdoors if you have room. However, you must not waste garden space on home-grown fruit trees in anticipation of getting a worthwhile crop from them in the future. The odds are much against them bearing the slighest resemblance to their parents and they will probably be absolutely useless. It's worth remembering that according to some botanists the crab-apple trees in our hedgerows are only rarely the native wild crab; most of them are wildings from cultivated apples whose pips have been swallowed by birds. The exception to this general uselessness of pip-grown fruit trees is the peach, which quite often turns up trumps and produces a better and more heavily-cropping tree than you will buy at the nurseryman's.

Repotting of trees should always be done when they are dormant and they should not be hurried into growth immediately after it. The seedling can remain in soil-less compost for its first season, and if transferred to JI 2 during the second winter it will need no further repotting for up to three years. By which time you will have replaced it.

Nothing of the above applies to *bonsai* trees, which are a law unto themselves. We shall come to them later.

Species Worth Growing

Seeds of most of the following are abundant in their season and not too slow or erratic in germinating. Though even the best-behaved in that context is not exactly comparable with mustard and cress.

Apple. Choose the pips from fully-ripe fruit. If the seed cannot be stratified the best results will come from long-keeping varieties used at the end of the season. Pips may be from dessert or culinary varieties. Plant in soil-less potting compost, covering seed half an inch deep, or in Jiffy 7s. Pips may also be planted in pots containing house plants as suggested for those of the citrus family; they must be moved to their own small pots as soon as they germinate. Germination time: three to eight weeks.

Ash. The ash seeds itself very freely, the twin seeds in their winged pods being borne far and wide on the wind. You can usually scoop them up by the handful anywhere in the vicinity of a parent tree. The number of ash seedlings that appear suggests that germination is usually good. It is fairly quick, too, for the little ash plants have time to grow into recognisable saplings in their first summer. The seed benefits from winter exposure and can be sown indoors in February. Remove the decaying wings and sow fairly thickly, half an inch deep. Seedlings should appear in two to four weeks, and the best ones are pricked out into 3" pots. The foliage of the ash is more decorative than is generally realised, but it does tend to become a very 'leggy' creature. Cut it back hard in the winter and persuade it to make several stems instead of one.

Beech. The hard-shelled edible fruit ('beechmast' which was once important as pig-food) will germinate better after a full winter's exposure. It may be that a spring ramble in a beechwood will lead to the discovery of some as yet uneaten nuts under the leaves. They will probably be ready to germinate if sown as soon as collected, but if they seem very dry and hard soak them for forty-eight hours. Treatment is the same as for apples. Sown in March, germination will be any time from April to July.

Cherry. Cherry stones are among those which are said to germinate only after passing through the digestive tract of a bird. Fortunately, this isn't true, but because the cherry ripens in high summer the seed is accustomed to a long wait before germinating the following spring – though no doubt the seedlings sometimes appear in autumn. One thing is certain, the cherry stone will not in its wild state ever be stored away in a drawer. It will be lying around on or in the soil.

Probably the best way of dealing with cherry stones is to push them into the compost of any house plants that have a little vacant soil space to spare. Use quite a few stones, preferably of different varieties and, unnecessary as the warning may appear, don't plant those left over from the cherry pie. I haven't a clue as to when cherry treelets will become apparent, but a safe guess would be some time between October and April. Just forget the stones are there and keep the pot plants watered as usual.

Chestnut. The fruit of the horse chestnut is a rewarding subject. It germinates easily – I have seen a compost heap onto which autumn sweepings were thrown thickly studded with young chestnut trees the following summer. The seed needs a winter rest, though, and the sand-in-a-tin method is the safest. If you have collected a load of conkers and don't mind losing a few, you can simply scoop a shallow hole in the garden, tip them in, cover with a few inches of soil and leave them till April.

When the chestnuts are dug up, or removed from the tin, some may already be showing signs of sprouting. Whether they are or not, plant them one inch deep in any type of potting compost in $4\frac{1}{2}''$ or $5''$ pots to avoid the necessity of potting-on the fast growing seedlings. Plant three chestnuts close together in the centre of the pot, this should ensure at least one seedling will result. If more than one appears, remove the surplus, leaving only the strongest. It will make an effective pot plant even during its first season, but after its second birthday may become too large. The chestnut is not really suitable for miniature dish gardens or for *bonsai*.

A horse chestnut seedling. These little trees make attractive summer pot plants.

Hawthorn. The scented flowers and clustered red berries of may, hawthorn or whitethorn are found everywhere outside purely urban areas. Little hawthorn trees – and the plant will attain the status of a small tree if left to grow unchecked – are nothing very special to look at, but they can be continuously pruned and kept very small. This makes them useful in the miniature garden and 'naturals' for *bonsai*. A hawthorn can be induced to look gnarled and aged while still quite young and very small.

Hawthorn berries, or rather the seeds inside them, germinate freely, and thousands of miles of hedgerow have in the past been planted with seedlings. But there is one snag; the berries need to be left for a *year* before being sown. Usual nursery practice is to sow in open ground in November those berries collected the previous autumn. This is too slow for most of us, and fair results could probably be obtained a little more quickly. Collect a handful of berries as late as possible in the winter; they are among the last to be eaten by birds and a few often survive until spring. Put them in the box of sand until the weather begins to warm up in April, then sow them indoors. Sow thickly in a pot or half-pot of soil-less compost, covering the berries to a depth of half an inch. Keep the pot at ordinary room temperature and covered with a piece of cardboard until germination starts. The compost must always be moist, and the cardboard should be removed at the first sign of germination. When this will be is anybody's guess. Probably about midsummer, and thereafter sporadically through the autumn.

As soon as the seedling is big enough to handle, prick it out into a small pot. Seedlings intended for *bonsai* should be moved to Jiffy pots or other peat pots filled with a JI compost. Peat pots are preferred for them because you need a pot whose sides the tree roots can penetrate.

Oak. Acorns should be collected as early as possible in the autumn, before the various feathered and four-legged collectors have had them all. Leave them outdoors in the sand-box until February, when they should be ready to germinate indoors.

Like avocado stones, acorns can be germinated in water, using a bottle filled right up and fitting the acorn fat end down into its neck like a cork. The method is not likely to commend itself to anyone but children, and the difficulty of finding bottles with precisely acorn-sized necks is considerable. It is less trouble to plant the acorns in pairs in small Jiffy pots, scrapping one seedling if both germinate. The acorns should be about an inch deep and the compost kept very moist, the pots being covered with

Acorns may be germinated like avocado stones – if you can find a bottle with a small enough neck.

A seedling oak. Baby oak trees, slow-growing and often keeping their leaves in winter, are useful in mini-gardens.

polythene and cardboard. Germination will take three to eight weeks.

Baby oaks are very slow-growing and splendid trees for the mini-garden. The fact that the old leaves often hang on until the new ones unfurl is an added advantage. They must have all the light possible if they are to remain compact and healthy.

Peach. Peach stones usually sprout without having to be wintered outdoors, though something has to be done about the very hard shell. Save the stones only from peaches that are dead ripe and soak them for forty-eight hours. If the shells are still hard, crack them very carefully, avoiding damage to the seed inside. The crack only has to be big enough to permit moisture in the compost to penetrate.

Plant in small pots of soil-less compost, one inch deep, and cover with polythene or place in a propagator. The use of individual peat pots is worth while, even if some remain treeless and have eventually to be put to another use. Of all fruit trees the peach has always seemed to me the most intolerant of root disturbance. In other words, it hates being moved. In a peat pot you can shift it to a larger size or a decorative container without it knowing what's happened.

Young peach trees are fast-growing, free-branching and quite decorative. Like the other stone fruit, they are useless for *bonsai*, but a tree which you no longer want indoors can be planted against a wall in your garden or given to a friend. There is a reasonable chance that it will fruit, and an outside one that you will hit the jackpot. I once heard of a seed-grown peach that produced nine hundred ripe fruit in a season, but exaggeration is endemic among gardeners, as it is among anglers.

*Second-year
peach seedling. A
dainty and poten-
tially useful tree.*

Pear. Same as for apple. Use pips from home-grown fruit at the end of their season.

Plum. Plum stones can be treated like those of the peach, but germinate better if wintered outdoors. In either case, the shell should be cracked if it is still hard.

Sycamore. The young sycamore is a very effective pot plant, with broad, well-shaped palmate leaves and a fairly compact habit when kept in full light. The winged 'keys' should be treated like those of the ash and should germinate fairly quickly if kept in sand for the winter and sown in early spring. The

*Young sycamore. Another
very decorative pot plant.*

tree is what foresters call a 'freely regenerating'
species, which means that it produces lots of seedlings.

The sycamore and the chestnut are probably the
two most attractive of our hardy tree seedlings, and
luckily they are among the easiest to grow.

6 Bonsai for Beginners

The sort of trees described in the last chapter make admirable pot plants for a year or two, but eventually they lose their attractiveness. They become tall and straggly, with too much wood and too little leaf, and eventually they have to be expelled from the house.

Large-growing trees can only be kept as permanent occupants of containers if they are dwarfed. The art of tree-dwarfing started in China, though the Japanese perfected it under the name of *bonsai*. Much time and patience is required to produce mature specimens, for the most valuable trees are those that look old and gnarled and picturesquely contorted. A tree has to be quite old in terms of years before this is achieved, even though it may be only a matter of inches high.

The time factor makes good bonsai very expensive to purchase, for they are not regarded as saleable until about six years old, when the initial training will have laid down the main shape of trunk and branches. A glance through the catalogue of a famous supplier shows that whereas trees of about eight years old may be bought for a few pounds, a foot-high conifer aged 130 will set you back £180. There is truly a lifetime's interest in this hobby, and, if you should become proficient at it, presumably a long-term investment for you and your descendants.

The miniature trees offered for sale are most usually conifers. The juniper, which is long-lived

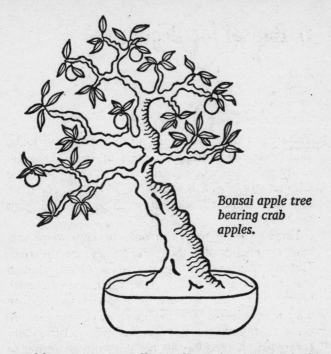

Bonsai apple tree bearing crab apples.

and has many naturally small species, is a particular favourite. However, a number of deciduous trees are traditionally used, and although they have not the year-round foliage of conifers there is the compensation of spring greenery and the fantastic structural shapes of trunk and limb displayed in winter if the tree is rested in a cool room.

The technique of bonsai can be practised on some of the species mentioned in Chapter Five, and even if you fail at first you can raise some more seedlings and try again – a less inhibiting situation than experimenting on expensive bought conifers. Of your seed and pip-grown trees, oak, sycamore, apple, and hawthorn are all good material. Of the stone fruits, plum is out because of its dislike of continual prun-

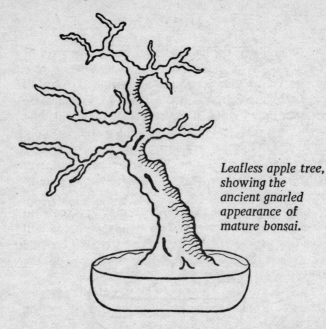

Leafless apple tree, showing the ancient gnarled appearance of mature bonsai.

ing, and the cherry and the peach are more usually grown as miniatures. The peach especially doesn't mind being cut back, but it is an energetic sprouter and you have to be ruthless with it to avoid a crowded bush rather than a tree.

Occasionally one can find and bring home a tiny seedling, an oak from woodland or a hawthorn from the shelter of a tall hedge. Very often the seed will have germinated in a strange or cramped situation, and the first few inches of stem will be distorted or slanting. Such a deformed seedling is worth its weight in gold to the bonsai enthusiast and should be carefully lifted and potted up.

Now, having a small tree whose impulse is to become a large one, you have to get it used to being miniaturised.

THE FIRST YEAR

The general effect of cutting back the top growth of any plant is to make it grow faster; every rose grower knows that weaklings are pruned heavily to encourage more shoots while rampant varieties are cut back only lightly in the hope that they will slow down. When it comes to persuading a tree virtually to stop growing at, say, one-fortieth of its proper height, and yet remain healthy and renew its leaves and minor branches, this tendency becomes a nuisance.

Merely to keep shortening or removing shoots on a young tree under normal growing conditions will have one of two results. Either the tree will become an uncontrollable thicket, or it will give up the struggle and peg out.

This explains why the seedling tree must be accustomed to a more restricted way of life before the serious training and cutting back begins. The first step is to slow down its growth rate by root pruning.

The Seedling

The seed or pip should be sown in a pot that makes it easy to get at the roots, or the little tree you've dug up should be planted in one. A Jiffy 7 or a small peat pot is probably the handiest; the roots soon grow out through the sides and bottom and must be regularly snipped off with sharp scissors. This continues for the first growing season. The top is allowed to grow naturally. The seedling is kept well watered but is not given any sort of feed; if by a year old it looks cramped and half-starved, that's fine.

Peat pots have a possible disadvantage in that they may begin to collapse after a time, but the thing to do then is to peel away the pot and put the seedling in another of the same size; this is not likely to happen with the Jiffy 7.

There is an alternative to the use of peat pots which will appeal to the economy-minded. Assuming that you have cut a grapefruit in half, eaten what is edible, and sown the pips, you can grow trees in the empty shells. Scrape the insides clean and dry them before the fire or on a radiator until the rind begins to shrink and feels lighter. Fill with compost and sow a few seeds or pips in the usual way, eventually reducing the seedlings to one. When this starts to grow, place the grapefruit 'pot' in a bowl of slightly moist peat. This not only reduces the amount of watering necessary but softens the skin and entices the seedling's roots to grow through it. At intervals it may be lifted out of the peat for inspection and the roots cut back. An orange can be used for the same purpose, but the half-orange skin is rather small.

If the seedling of a deciduous tree has germinated in spring and made some inches of top during the summer you may have been able to cut back its roots several times during that period. In that case you can transfer it to a small ordinary pot in the autumn when its leaves fall. A 3″ pot will be large enough and it should be kept in the coolest possible place and watered only enough to stop the compost drying out.

If the tree started late in the season and has made little first-year growth, leave it in the peat pot and carry on snipping back its roots all through the following summer.

Training

With the young tree established in its first perma-

nent container, and its growth slowed down by root
pruning, you can begin to think about shaping it.
But first, a word about containers and composts.

A well-chosen decorative container makes a lot of
difference to the tree's appearance, though during
the first year or two, when the tree is handled a good
deal, with a consequently greater risk of breakage,
it is wise to use only an ordinary flower pot. Whatever is used, it must have drainage holes, and it
should be small in relation to the size of the tree.
This last proviso may seem a nuisance when you
have produced a tree with a semi-recumbent trunk
and the sprawling, windswept look which bonsai enthusiasts seem to delight in. Such a tree looks out of
place in a small conventionally-shaped pot, but if
you plant it in a larger one its root-run will no longer be restricted and the dwarfing effects will be lost.
This is why professionally produced bonsai are often
planted in dish-shaped containers, where they look
right but have little root space because the container
is shallow. Incidentally, I'm told that the word *bonsai* means 'growing in shallow ground', but I cannot
vouch for this.

A too-large container can always have its capacity
reduced by a few partially buried lumps of rock.
These also look well, especially when a woody root
comes to the surface among them to give the impres-
sion of an ancient tree in a harsh landscape. Bonsai
may be planted in miniature gardens, but only if
they are left in small pots which can be completely
buried. To plant the tree directly in the garden is to
court disaster for both; the roots will take over and
starve the other occupants, and the tree will become
an unwelcome Gulliver in Lilliput. Even when kept
in its pot you will have to dig it up now and then to
clip off the roots escaping from the drainage hole.

The compost requirements of bonsai are very simple. JIP 1 is as good as anything, or you can make up a mixture of two parts good loam, one part peat, and one part coarse sand, without worrying about the loam being sterilised. Weeds will appear for a time but will do no harm and are easily removable. A little bone meal and hoof-and-horn meal – very slow-acting fertilisers – should be mixed into the compost. A sprinkling of them can also be given once a year to established trees, lightly stirred into the top of the soil. Soil-less compost is not suitable for bonsai except in the early stages. It involves more frequent repotting.

On no account should bonsai be given regular feeds of liquid fertilisers with a high nitrogen content.

The shaping of the tree is something calling for a good visual sense and some manual dexterity. From the start you need a clear picture in your own mind of how the tree should ultimately look. Is it to be a miniature replica of a perfect adult of its own species, Tall and columnar or squat and spreading? Exactly symmetrical or grotesquely lopsided? Whatever you decide you must work consistently to attain. Where a branch is going to be needed, there a shoot must be allowed to grow; if a branch at that point has no place in the design the shoot must be promptly cut back. If a twig is growing in the wrong direction to form the branch you want at that particular point you must change its direction, remembering that 'as the twig is bent, so will the branch grow'.

The pruning – the cutting away of unwanted growth – can be done with sharp scissors, preferably small and pointed, or with a razor blade. The latter can make a very clean job but must be handled with care to avoid removing more than intended – including small portions of oneself. The important thing is that the shoot or twig should be cut back flush with the stem from which it originates, so that a spur or stump is left. This sounds simple to achieve, but in fact requires quite a bit of care and practice.

At first you will allow the main stem or trunk and the laterals springing from it to grow naturally. Then you may find there is not enough bare trunk at the bottom and some of the lower laterals must be removed altogether. When some of the remaining branches have spread as far horizontally as you want they are stopped by having the leading shoots nipped off. From that point onwards more sub-laterals will develop on the stopped branch, and these must not be allowed to grow into a thicket of twigs. Cut out the unwanted ones every few months, but don't be perpetually snipping. The tree will not benefit by having you perpetually hovering around, scissors in hand, like a well-meaning Sweeney Todd. And as it ages the amount of pruning necessary will diminish if you have slowed down its growth rate by limiting the root system.

To train the tree into the desired shape – and form is all important in bonsai – you have to change the look of branches as well as remove them. You may even want to alter the angle at which the trunk is growing.

This is done by attaching a training wire to the trunk or the particular limb and exerting a pull by gradually tightening the wire. If, for example, you find a twig which you have selected to form a horizontal bough growing persistently in an upward direction, you slowly pull it down by means of the wire until it grows in the right position with no tendency to spring back. This often has to be done a little at a time over a long period; too great a haste may break the branch.

Soft copper wire, plastic coated, is good for the purpose. A wire that is easily bent and not springy is necessary if you are to wrap it round comparatively tender growths without breakage. It should also be inconspicuous in colour because the tree may have to wear training wires for several years.

The wire can be attached to the branch by simply twisting it round several times, without making a tight loop which may cut into the bark. It is then led down to a tethering point from which a pull in the right direction can be obtained. The periodic tightening of the wire can be done in two ways. It can be undone and pulled tighter at the end, which is fiddling and difficult to control exactly. A better way is to make a small loop in the wire midway between the branch and the anchorage point. You then have only to twist the loop a few more times whenever you want a slight additional pull.

The end of the wire can sometimes be fastened round the base of the trunk itself when a direct downward pull is needed, but this cannot be done when it is the trunk that has to be pulled, or when a branch needs to be directed sideways. The neatest arrangement is to make some provision for fastening the training wires to the rim of the container, and if this is still an ordinary flower pot it can be managed fairly inconspicuously. A plastic pot can have small holes drilled at intervals round the rim, about half an inch below the top, through which the wires can be threaded. For an earthenware pot, select one which has a thickened rim, and encircle it with a tightly-bound wire just below the rim. The training wires can then be tied to this and the pull exerted in almost any direction.

General Management

After a few years the bonsai should be unmistakably a tree, complete with trunk, bark, branches, twigs and leaves. If you have mastered the trick of reducing its growth-rate by root pruning it will remain healthy and actively growing while no more than a tiny fraction of the normal size of its species. That's the final object of the exercise – a mature, perfect tree in a dish or bowl.

It must always be remembered, though, that such a home-grown tree is completely hardy, and that the more time it can spend in the open air, or on a sill by an open window, the better. All deciduous trees must rest in winter, but your bonsai cannot be left out in frost. Not because it will kill the tree, but because it may burst the container. Keep it over the winter in an unheated room or garden shed or garage. Remember to keep the compost damp but not wet. This banishment need be only of about three months' duration – you can bring it back into the warmth of the living room about February and provide it with an early spring. A good rule in the summer is to stand the tree outdoors in a partially shaded position for three days a week. Indoors, give it the lightest position you can, and one away from artificial heat.

Watering may be necessary once a day in the growing season, especially if the tree gets a lot of sun. Occasional overhead watering in the evening from a fine rose is as good for the foliage as summer rain, but however the water is given there must always be enough of it to percolate right through the compost and trickle out of the drainage holes.

7 Some very Pippy Ones

The subjects of this chapter produce small seeds in large numbers. This gives you a chance to overcome poor germination percentages by sowing a lot of pips.

These three fruits, the grape, the lychee, and the pomegranate, are all eaten in this country, but their popularity ratings are very different. Everyone eats grapes at some time, even if only in hospital (where the opportunities for pip-growing are limited). The lychee has been slow to spread beyond its native China, but has now become popular in many parts of the world and is cultivated widely in warm temperate and sub-tropical climates. Pomegranates are something of an acquired taste, and one which I am never likely to acquire; more to our purpose, they can be grown as most attractive shrubs and have long been used for greenhouse decoration.

In general, the seeds saved from these fruits are treated like those of any greenhouse or half-hardy species. They are sown in warmth, in shallow pans or trays of seed compost, and pricked out into small pots for growing on. It is worth sowing as many seeds as you can collect, even if this means sowing very thickly. Germination in all of them is an uncertain factor, but at least a few seedlings should always emerge from a generous sowing, and even one plant of any of these three is a real acquisition.

THE GRAPE

Grape pips may be sown immediately the fruit is eaten, or washed, dried and stored for a time to accumulate more. On the whole, it is better to sow them fresh, and although the number of pips varies with the variety of grape you will probably find that the residue of a pound of grapes gives you plenty for a first attempt. There is no precise season for sowing but late winter or early spring means the optimum conditions for the seedlings.

Sow in a pan or half-pot of soil-less compost, spacing out the pips as evenly as you can and covering them only very lightly – just enough to make sure that none of them is visible when you give a gentle watering after sowing to settle the compost over them.

Place the pan in a propagator or cover it with polythene and paper. Keep it in a reasonably warm spot, but a lot of heat is not needed and will do little to hasten germination. The grape, unlike many of the fruit whose pips concern us here, is not a native of the tropics.

Germination will take at least two or three weeks and will be very erratic, one or two seedlings popping up at intervals. When the first appears the paper covering must be removed and the seedlings given full light. As each one gets big enough to manipulate, transfer it carefully to a 3" pot. You may ultimately move it to a larger size, but don't do so for a year. In fact your little grape vine can stay in a small pot for as long as you keep it.

These miniature vines are highly decorative and worth a little perseverance to obtain. They can be trained up canes or up the side of the window frame. They need a winter rest in a cool room after the

Young seedling grape vine. May be planted in the open when no longer wanted indoors.

leaves fall, when watering is reduced to a minimum. If kept in a cool room before leaf-fall, or left outside for a few weeks in early autumn there is always a chance of getting red and gold coloration in the foliage. This is not certain, because no-one can know what sort of vine a seed will produce, though it is far more likely to be attractive in appearance than it is to bear edible grapes. Incidentally, too few people realise what a vigorous and beautiful garden climber an ornamental vine can be, covering sheds and fences and blazing into crimson in the autumn.

Indoor vines need all the light they can get, and frequent watering in the summer if in a small pot. After a couple of years they may begin to look

rather stiff and woody and can then be planted outdoors and replaced by new seedlings. The chances
are that any vine raised from a pip will be hardier
than most named varieties of grape.

A particularly attractive vine can be propagated
by layering. Plant it in a large half-pot, so that there
is a surrounding area of bare compost. In the spring,
as the leaf buds are about to develop, lay as much
of the vine as possible flat on the compost. Make
sure that some of the buds are firmly in contact with
it by placing small stones on the stem close to them.
Keep the surface moist throughout the summer and
by autumn a number of these buds should have
sprouted both roots and lateral shoots. Cut the original stem and pot them up separately.

THE LYCHEE

It should really be the lichee or litchee – to rhyme
with itchy – for its botanical name is Litchi *chinensis*. But lychee seems to be generally accepted.

In China, where the lychee has been cultivated
for more than 2,000 years, it is more popular than
either the orange or the peach. Nowhere does it
grow wild, an indication of its great popularity over
a long period.

The tree is unusually beautiful for a commercial
fruit. It is a symmetrically-growing evergreen, the
pinnate leaves being a glossy green, though in the
spring the young foliage, which then predominates,
is an orange-red. Although it is thought to have come
to China from tropical Malaya, the lychee is now
exported from much cooler places such as New Zealand and South Africa. When grown in this country
it must have a good deal of warmth in the early

stages, but once established would need only the same room temperature as most house plants and could stand outdoors in summer. It is slow growing, and for pot culture this is an advantage. Regrettably, a seedling takes about ten years to reach fruiting age, so you are unlikely to pick fruit. As with our own fruit trees, lychees raised from seed are said to bear inferior or worthless fruit.

The fruit of the lychee is only about an inch in diameter and slightly more than that in length. The correct method of eating is to slice off one end as one does the top of an egg, place that end in the mouth, and squeeze. The white, fragrant flesh is comparable in flavour with the muscat grape. The seed is easily separated from the flesh and a considerable quantity will have been collected by the time the lychee-eater has had a satisfying intake.

The seed has a peculiarity which makes it pretty certain that you will never be able to buy a packet of lychee seed at the garden shop; it loses its viability within a few days of being removed from the fruit. Even within the fruit it stays viable for only a matter of weeks. And the moral of this is to eat your lychees as soon as you get them and sow the pips as fast as you can spit them out.

Treat them as you did the grape seeds, but provide them with maximum warmth. Germination should take place in about two weeks and the compost must be kept really moist before and after the emergence of the seedlings. The latter are at first rather delicate, disliking violent changes in temperature and preferring a light but shady situation to a sunny window sill. They are perfectly alright in full sun after a few months, but at all stages must have plenty of water.

Not only does the lychee thrive in naturally moist

soils, it also likes acid ones containing a high pro-
portion of peat. For this reason the best compost for
the lychee is probably a soil-less one designed for
lime-haters like azaleas. This type of compost is as
easily obtainable as the standard variety if you ask
for it at the garden shop. The lychee will grow quite
well in a more alkaline soil such as JIP 2, but if your
tap water is very hard it will benefit from being
watered with rainwater.

A 5″ pot will be large enough for a year or two,
but when the lychee reaches shrub size it will be
worthy of a considerably larger container.

THE POMEGRANATE

This fruit, consisting mainly of skin, pips and juice,
has been cultivated for all historical time. The Israel-
ites, wandering in the wilderness, recalled refreshing
themselves with it when they were slaves in Egypt.
It was the apple of discord that Paris gave to Venus,
and is an ancient fertility symbol.

For the ardent pip grower the pomegranate is a
rich source of raw material; it must surely be the
pippiest fruit in cultivation, not even excepting the
blackberry and raspberry. It is about the size of an
apple and its tough rind encloses the seeds, some
pulp, and a great deal of refreshing juice. This is
thought by some people to be unique among fruit
juices, and apart from its distinctive flavour it is
supposedly 'good for you'. The Prophet Mohammed
said 'Eat the pomegranate, it purges the system of
envy and hatred', and quite recently the juice has
been found to have anti-bacterial qualities.

All this is by the way, though it may encourage
you to try some pomegranates for reasons other

than pip-collecting. What really concerns us is the pomegranate tree or shrub; its maximum height is only about fifteen feet so it might be described as either. In a sheltered place in this country it will live outdoors and was first grown here in 1548 at Syon House. When grown in a border or a large pot in a greenhouse it can even be induced to ripen fruit.

Purely for decoration it was once popular, and this popularity seems to be returning. A new dwarf form, Punica *granatum nana*, has been bred purely as a pot plant, bearing tiny golden fruit. However, the standard variety, grown from home-saved pips, is also an attractive plant, though less compact and slower in growth. It is semi-deciduous, losing most of its leaves in the winter of a cool climate, but retaining them in a tropical one. The flowers are tubular, with convoluted petals of brilliant scarlet. They start to open in the late spring and may continue well into the summer. The tree is somewhat unusual in carrying both hermaphrodite and male blossoms, only the former, of course, forming fruit.

The actual tree is about as hardy as the peach and withstands quite severe frost. The seed needs a temperature of about 70°F (21°C) for germination and spring is the best time to sow it. It is possible to wash and dry the seed, storing it for some time, and the entire fruit can also be kept without deterioration for some weeks. The skin may shrink and become brittle and the flavour is said to improve. The seed becomes tender and edible, and may possibly germinate more readily after being kept in the fruit than when stored dry.

Actual sowing is as for any small seed. Cover it only lightly with compost and inspect daily to make sure that it is moist. This is always more important with seeds near the surface than with those planted deeper, and soil-less compost can sometimes look damper than it really is.

Prick out the seedlings into small peat pots and grow them on in a sunny position. Move to a larger pot when roots begin to penetrate the sides. The young pomegranate dislikes being shunted around, and the peat pot makes transplanting easier.

A large pot or small tub may eventually be needed for the pomegranate. It is completely unfussy over soil, and if a JIP compost is used repotting will not often be necessary. For the first year or two, when the plant needs a frequent move to a larger pot size, soil-less compost can be used.

Plenty of water is needed in summer, especially for a large shrub standing outdoors in a sunny position. A fortnightly dose of liquid fertiliser at this time of year will increase growth and prolong the blossoming season.

An established pomegranate can be propagated by cuttings, a much quicker process than raising fresh seedlings. Choice of the right material for cuttings is important, and the best ones come from the basal suckers.

I referred to the pomegranate as a tree or shrub. Commercially, it would probably be grown as a tree, with a single stem and spreading top. Left to grow naturally it produces suckers round the base of the main stem, giving it more of a bushy shape. From the decorative point of view it looks nicer like this, and some of these secondary stems should always be left to grow. They also provide the best cuttings, provided they are long enough and about a year old.

Take the cuttings in spring from the previous year's growth. They should be about nine inches long and cut just below a leaf-joint. They will of course be tip cuttings, the upper part of the sucker stem, with some large leaves and probably some smaller ones at the top. All the larger leaves are removed, only a little tuft at the top being left. The cuttings are inserted some three inches deep in a rooting medium such as a mixture of soil-less compost and coarse sand and enclosed in the usual polythene bag or propagator. Keep well watered and in warmth but out of direct sun.

The pomegranate joins the peach in being one of the few fruit trees which may well produce edible fruit of good quality when raised from seed. Unlike the peach it has no hope of doing so in the garden, but if you have a warm greenhouse with plenty of head-room you might achieve something quite spectacular.

8 Loquats, Kumquats and Kiwis

You may not be familiar with them, and they are not to be found in every fruiterer's. But the kiwi is marketed here as the Chinese gooseberry; the loquat is imported and well known to those who holiday in the Mediterranean area, while the kumquat is almost commonplace in the United States and is doubtless beginning to arrive here from Florida.

All are of interest to the pipster, and the kumquat especially is such a splendid pot plant that it would be worth importing a few solely for the pips. Because that's the only way you will ever be able to grow it.

THE LOQUAT

Not long ago I saw an enquiry in a gardening magazine from a reader who had brought back a furry-skinned fruit from Menorca and raised a plant from one of its pips. He didn't know what it was and was told it was a loquat.

Its popular name is Japanese medlar, which approximately indicates its area of origin. It is now grown all over the sub-tropical world and the fruit is increasingly used in Continental countries, not only for dessert but in preserves. The loquat fruit is oval, up to three inches in length, yellow or orange in colour, with a thin, downy skin. It is sweet and refreshing both raw and cooked. There are usually two or three pips and they are quite large, up to half an inch in length.

The loquat tree – or shrub, depending on conditions and treatment – has been grown in England since 1787. In Southern England it can be planted outdoors against a wall and will survive average winters, but is unlikely to produce eatable fruit when kept permanently outdoors. In the greenhouse it is as easy to fruit as a peach, and when grown as a pot plant for the house it can be treated like members of the citrus family and will flower and fruit in a pot or tub.

The foliage is impressive – perhaps even more so than that of the avocado. The dark green, corrugated leaves reach a length of ten inches or more when full-grown. The young leaves form a complete contrast to them, being grey-green, downy and altogether softer in appearance. The flowers are creamy-coloured and are borne in long panicles of perhaps fifty individual blossoms; usually only about a dozen of these form fruit and if more do so they should be thinned. The blossoms appear at intervals from November to April, so the loquat does not have a true resting period in winter. It must be kept in a reasonably warm room, say 50°F (10°C) or over, in the best-lighted position you can manage, and watered moderately. At all times of the year it benefits from having the foliage sprayed with tepid water.

This habit of flowering in winter explains why there is little hope of fruiting the loquat outdoors in this country; a slight frost, harmless to the shrub itself, is enough to destroy the blossoms or young fruit. Given protection during this vital period the loquat in its pot may be placed outdoors in a sunny position from May onwards. An unheated greenhouse or a sunny garden room is even better, both for ripening the fruit and for producing the strong new shoots which will blossom the following winter. This of course applies equally to the citruses and others of our pip-begotten fruit trees – not that they have the same annual cycle as the loquat, but they all benefit from maximum sunlight and warmth in the summer.

Propagation and Pruning

The pips are best planted in April or May, when very little artificial warmth is needed. Although quite large they should only be covered to a depth of half an inch. Germination takes at least three weeks and the seedlings should be treated like those of the citrus fruits.

It is advisable not to store the seeds for too long, and any brought back from a summer holiday in the Med. should be planted right away and not put aside until the following spring.

Cuttings may be taken in August, but they have the reputation of being difficult to root. An easier way of multiplying an established loquat is by layering the lower branches. The spreading, shrub-like growth makes this simpler by producing nice little horizontal branches low on the stem. One or more of these is bent down in the spring on to a pot or deep tray of compost, the point of contact being a leaf joint, and is held down by a weight of some sort. A small diagonal cut may be made on the underside of the branch to encourage root formation, but this is not essential. A little compost should be heaped over the branches where it touches and all should be regularly watered and never allowed to dry out – this would destroy any developing roots. The branch should have rooted before the end of the summer and may be cut from the main stem and potted up. It can be trimmed in such a way that any laterals growing upwards are left as main stems.

The pruning of the pot-grown loquat is aimed at keeping it as small and bushy as possible. When it reaches a height of three feet the leader is 'headed back'. The horizontal branches will then grow faster and they too may have to be tipped.

Root pruning is also a help in controlling the loquat's growth and in promoting earlier maturity. When repotting you may discover a thick tap root coiled round at the bottom of the pot, or unusually fleshy roots pressed against the pot's sides. These should be cut off cleanly level with the outside of the soil ball, but care must be taken not to sacrifice the smaller fibrous roots.

THE KUMQUAT

Commercial growers still look on the kumquat as a citrus fruit. Botanists also thought it was until a century ago, when the explorer and plant-hunter Robert Fortune told them it wasn't. It was re-named Fortunella, and there are several edible species. The two best known are Marumi and Nagami, Japanese names which are familiar to American shoppers. They are grown in Florida and classed as a sort of very small orange blessed with a rind that can be eaten uncooked. This rind is thick, sweet, and has the same flavour as the pulp; the fruit is round or oval, only about an inch in diameter, and may be preserved in syrup as well as eaten fresh.

The shrub – it hardly reaches the dimensions of a tree even in a sub-tropical climate – is an evergreen and very similar to the true citrus species. Of all this large group it is perhaps the nearest to being an ideal pot plant. The general effect is that of a very small, compact orange tree, though the leaves are a darker green and every part of the shrub is scented. The flowers are white, smaller than those of the orange, and appear during spring and summer.

The kumquat is resistant to cold and can stand lower temperatures than the orange. In spite of this it pays to keep it in a light and fairly warm room through the winter, one which remains above 55°F (13°C) being ideal, and to keep it growing instead of allowing it to go to sleep. One reason for the kumquat's relative hardiness is that its growth stops completely at temperatures around 50°F (10°C) and the leaves and shoots become tougher. But you want growth in the very early spring to produce early blooms and so give the fruits time to mature and ripen in late summer and autumn. Not only does this make it possible to pick ripe fruit at Christmas, the quality is improved by the fact that it developed during the warmest months of the year.

Planting

This must be done whenever you can get hold of the pips. They should if possible be planted immediately after removal from the fruit, when germination is good and fairly rapid. Chances of success diminish with the length of time the seed is stored. All the same, if you cannot find kumquats for sale here and an American friend offers to send you some, accept with gratitude. Just ask him to transfer the pips from the fruit to a sealed polythene envelope and airmail it.

The pips are planted like those of the citrus family, covered not more than half an inch deep, and will germinate readily in a temperature of 60°F

(16°C). In winter they are safer in some kind of propagator, but when planted in spring or summer a warm window sill is better. The seedlings dislike a close humid atmosphere and should not be over-watered. The pips are another suitable subject for starting in the pots of existing house plants, but if you have only a few to play with they are better in individual peat pots or Jiffy 7s. After a year or two in medium size pots and soil-less compost they should be moved to successively larger sizes and JIP 3. Nothing larger than a 12″ pot should be needed, even for a fruiting shrub.

The care in watering needed for the seedlings should be applied to older plants. In winter the amount of water given depends on how quickly the plant is growing; the compost must not be allowed to dry out as much as would be permissible for a completely dormant tree – it should always be uniformly moist. In summer, so long as the pot is well-drained, the kumquat likes plenty of water at the roots and regular overhead spraying in hot weather. A fortnightly feed of a liquid fertiliser with a high potash content (ask your garden shop) is worthwhile once the little shrub starts fruiting.

THE KIWI FRUIT

At the time when I first encountered this it was universally known as the Chinese gooseberry. It came to be nicknamed the kiwi because, apart from China, its main centre of cultivation is New Zealand.

The Chinese gooseberry, Actinidia *sinensis*, is a hardy, woody-stemmed, deciduous climber. In other words its way of life is much like that of clematis or honeysuckle. It was brought to this country in

1900, but is still virtually unknown here, the fruit being imported from New Zealand.

There is absolutely no reason why anyone wanting an unusual climber, with the added bonus of edible fruits, should not grow kiwis up any convenient bit of wall or trellis. The hardiness of the plant is emphasised by the names of two of its near relatives, the Manchurian gooseberry and the Siberian gooseberry. It will grow on any soil and in either sun or shade, but full sun is necessary to ripen and flavour the fruit.

This fruit is about the size and shape of a very large gooseberry, enclosed in a tough skin covered with reddish hairs. This peels off easily when the fruit is ripe, and the firm green flesh has something of the flavour of a dessert gooseberry. It may be eaten like any other fresh fruit or used in a variety of ways – sliced and used as a substitute for angelica in decoration for instance.

Actinidia is obviously not a pot plant, though up to two years old it could provide an indoor climber like the grape vine – though less attractive. The real purpose in sowing the pips is to produce a novel climber for garden or courtyard, for if you want a kiwi you'll almost certainly have to hatch your own.

In fact, if you want fruit you will have to plant several seedlings; the species is unisexual and the fruit on a female plant will not develop without a male pollinator nearby. The flowers are creamy white, and a full-grown vine with the flower tassels set off by the dark green heart-shaped leaves deserves acceptance as a purely ornamental plant.

Propagation

The pips of the Chinese gooseberry are small and not so easy to extract as those of some fruits. They may be sown fresh if this is convenient, but there seems no reason why they should not be dried and stored until the best sowing time, which is April.

A high temperature is not needed for germination, and a seed pan on the window sill, covered with glass or polythene, is all that you need. Sow as many seeds as you can collect, covering them only lightly. As soon as they can be handled the seedlings are pricked out into small pots and grown on either indoors or standing outside. One warning about plants in small pots outdoors: it is apt to be a case of 'out of sight, out of mind', and small pots dry out terribly quickly in sun and wind. It is safer to sink all pot plants in the ground to pot-rim level to keep the roots cool and reduce evaporation. You may have trouble with roots spreading out through the drainage holes but this will not become serious in only a few weeks or months.

Bring the young kiwis indoors in the autumn and keep them in a cool room or greenhouse, watering sparingly and moving them to larger pots before the new leaves appear in the spring. During that spring and summer they may be used as decorative climbers indoors and put in their permanent quarters outdoors in October.

Stem cuttings about four inches long may be taken in July or August if you want more plants, but the easiest form of vegetative propagation is by layering a length of stem in the autumn. Peg it down firmly and leave it for a year. Then, in the following autumn, cut it up and plant the rooted portions separately.

It may be that some nurserymen are offering plants of this attractive climber, but as far as I can ascertain the only way of getting it is via the pips of the kiwi fruit.

9 Gambler's Corner

Some of the plant-raising suggestions in this book have an element of uncertainty about them – not all will succeed at the first attempt. But so far everything considered is within the scope of everyday horticulture, and the odds against the amateur gardener are no greater than in attempting any other range of unfamiliar plants.

Because so many people think, quite wrongly, that growing plants from pips and other oddments is a wild gamble, it seems only fair to end with some ideas that are just that.

Here then are the rank outsiders, the long-shots where the professsionals often admit failure and the completely inexperienced have as good a chance as anyone.

GINGER

The dried root ginger used in cooking is strictly a rhizome or tuber like those of the dahlia or iris. It comes from a tropical Asiatic plant called Zingiber *officinale* (the specific name *officinale* or *officinalis* always means that a plant is or was used in the 'offices' – the kitchens). The Chinese, who must have been the world's bravest experimental eaters, were the first to cultivate and to export ginger. It was actually grown in this country as early as 1605 and featured as a decorative greenhouse curiosity in the last century.

Ginger plant. Only un-processed root ginger has the remotest chance of growing.

The plant is a perennial, dying down in the winter, when it needs a temperature of 55°F (13°C), and shooting up in the spring. It grows about three feet tall and the flower spike is quite impressive, nearly a foot long and a blend of purple and greenish-yellow.

In theory it is possible to propagate the ginger plant from the dried roots bought for flavouring, and if you have some among the spice jars I suggest you make the attempt. That experienced gardener, G. H. Witham Fogg, says in his delightful book *See How They Grow* that he has tried repeatedly without any result. I have never even tried. But a gentleman wrote to *The New York Times* in 1972 saying that he had planted bits of root ginger in the autumn and had some large plants by February. He wanted to know whether they would outgrow his apartment and if it was true that he could just cut a slice off the new rhizomes when he wanted ginger for his Chinese cooking. So it can be done.

The dried ginger 'roots', called 'hands' because of the way the rhizomes are grouped, are imported in two forms, coated and uncoated. The latter have been peeled and processed and are usually sold pre-packed; there is no hope of them growing. The un-coated roots are most likely to be sold by the tradi-tional non-supermarket grocer, and he may even be able to tell you something about their origins. This form of root is unpeeled and dried in the sun. If it hasn't been kicking around for too long there is al-ways the chance that it may sprout like any other dried tuber.

Plant the pieces of root close together in soil-less compost kept moist and as warm as possible. If noth-ing has happened after a couple of months, nothing will. You may feel that this is a shocking waste of ginger and wonder if you can still use the roots. Not, I'm afraid if they were in compost, because they have absorbed the nutrient fertilisers. If planted in vermiculite or pure peat you could presumably use them if they are still sound.

If a piece of rhizome does shoot it should be potted up separately and grown on in a warm room. The plant resents direct sunlight, and if the tempera-ture is reasonable will succeed in a north window. It needs plenty of water in spring and summer, but after October, when the leaves die off, the roots should be kept almost dry. The flower spike appears in July.

SWEET CHESTNUTS

The eating chestnut is not really a gamble, in fact it germinates more quickly than the horse chestnut. To which, incidentally, it is no relation. The only element of uncertainty is in the age of the nuts, which perform best when quite fresh. The ideal time to plant them is as soon as they are harvested, but as we can only plant things when they turn up in the home this is not likely to happen. Buy some nuts as soon as they appear, though, if you want to raise trees from them; the after-Christmas ones are a much more doubtful proposition.

Select plump-looking nuts with undamaged shells – the sort that look most worth eating – and plant them an inch deep in any sort of seed compost. Use a large half-pot and space them well apart so that the seedlings may be removed and potted up separately without root damage. They can also be planted in the open ground, but early Autumn planting is then even more important.

When grown indoors ordinary room temperature is high enough, and the pot should be covered to reduce the frequency of watering. The compost should be kept really moist.

The seedlings are treated like those of other hardy trees mentioned in this book and can be planted outdoors or given away when a year old. In fact the best thing you can do with them is to use them as prestige presents – 'Would you care for a few Spanish chestnut trees?' – for they are boring things with none of the beauty of the horse chestnut. Even as seedlings they are far less effective pot plants, lacking the large palmate leaves.

If you have several acres to be planted up with trees the sweet chestnut is very hardy and makes useful timber while young. As a final bit of useless information, you need 600 lb. of chestnuts to produce an acre of seedlings.

NUTMEGS

The nutmeg as we know it is the kernel of a nut, the outer shell having been removed. If the skin is hard, dark brown, and wrinkled this kernel should – again in theory – germinate. The causes of failure in growing nutmeg trees from them are probably twofold; first there is the loss of viability, for no-one can tell how long a nutmeg has been in store; second, there is loss of patience on the part of the grower. Even in its own climate the nutmeg takes three months to germinate, and this is an awful long time to go on watering an unresponsive nut.

Here I would make a suggestion to those planting up a bottle garden or terrarium. Why not plant in the compost a few hard shelled, slow-starting seeds of tropical origin, such as nutmegs, Brazil nuts (which come from a palm) and even date stones? The conditions would be right for them, especially if you were growing such warmth-loving subjects as Cryptanthus *acaulis*, Maranta *makoyna*, or Fittonia *argyroneura*. Germination would be so slow and infrequent that there would be no serious disturbance of the regular occupants from removal of any seedlings, and of course the buried seeds would need no special attention.

This would not be a suitable place to start other seeds suggested in the book, such as citrus pips and avocado stones, which germinate more quickly and need prompt attention and different surroundings to those of a bottle garden. It is put forward as another of those silly experiments which can add so much interest to any form of gardening, and which so often succeed because one never expects them to.

You might also plant a few sweet almonds at Christmas time; they have almost as good a chance as a peach stone and the young tree is of course very much like the peach.

But don't try to get a clove tree by sowing cloves, desirable as a specimen of that splendid tropical tree would be. The clove is merely a dried flower bud without a seed in it.

Appendix One

GLOSSARY OF SOME TERMS
USED IN THIS BOOK

Axil The angle formed by a leaf-stalk or petiole where it joins a stem. It often encloses an *axillary bud* capable of developing a flower or another stem.

Deciduous Applied particularly to trees which lose their leaves during the winter rest period. Other trees and shrubs are *semi-deciduous*, losing or retaining their leaves according to the temperature. *Evergreens* keep their foliage at all times, only dropping and replacing individual leaves.

Dormant Literally sleeping. A dormant plant, as during the winter rest period, requires much less water than one in active growth.

Lateral A branch growing out sideways from an existing stem. The growth of laterals is often stimulated by pinching out the growing point of the main stem, a method of changing the plant's habit of growth.

Leader   The growing shoot by which a stem or branch extends its length. Shortening a leader is described as *heading back*.

Leguminous A plant bearing its seeds in a pod or *legume*, of which both the pea and the peanut are examples. The flowers of the family are very distinctive, all having a broad upper petal, the *standard*, and four narrower ones forming the *wings* and *keel*.

Pot-bound A condition in which a container is so full of roots that a mass of them encloses the soil-ball. A pot-bound plant should have the matted roots slightly loosened before being transferred to a larger container with fresh compost.

Potting Up Transfer of a seedling from its place of germination to an individual pot. This should be done as soon as the seedling is big enough to handle and before it has made a lot of root. *Pricking out* is basically the same operation.

Seed-leaf The first leaf to emerge on germination. The seed-leaf or *cotyledon* is usually quite different in form to all the leaves which the plant will carry in future. All flowering trees and shrubs are *dicotyledonous* and have an identical pair of seed-leaves.

Species   A small natural group in the classification of living things. The group is a natural one because different varieties within it can interbreed. Similar species are themselves grouped in a *genus*, but this is an artificial arrangement and the different species cannot interbreed. Botanists sometimes switch plant species from one genus to another, which is confusing. The name of the genus is given first and specific name second. Thus the lemon is Citrus (genus) *limonia* (species).

Stop   To pinch out the growing point of a stem or branch in order to promote a more bushy type of growth.

Appendix Two

BOTANICAL NAMES OF THE PLANTS
IN THIS BOOK
For readers wishing to look them up in textbook
or catalogue.

ALMOND — Prunus amygdalus
APPLE — Pyrus malus
ASH — Fraxinus excelsior
AVOCADO — Persea gratissima
BEECH — Fagus sylvatica
BRAZIL NUT TREE — Bertholletia excelsa
CARROT — Daucus carota
CHERRY — Prunus avium
CHESTNUT, HORSE — Aesculus hippocastanum
CHESTNUT, SWEET — Castanea sativa
CHINESE GOOSEBERRY (KIWI FRUIT) — Actinidia
sinensis
COFFEE TREE — Coffea arabica
DATE PALM — Phoenix dactylifera
GINGER PLANT — Zingiber officinale
GRAPE — Vitis vinifera
GRAPEFRUIT — Citrus grandis or Citrus paradisi
HAWTHORN — Crataegus monogyna
KUMQUAT, MARUMI — Fortunella japonica
KUMQUAT, NAGAMI — Fortunella marharita
LEMON — Citrus limonia
LIME — Citrus aurantifolia
LOQUAT — Eriobotrya japonica
LYCHEE — Litchi chinensis

NUTMEG — Myristica fragrans
OAK — Quercus robur
ORANGE, MANDARIN — Citrus reticulata
ORANGE, SEVILLE — Citrus aurantium
ORANGE, SWEET — Citrus sinensis
PEACH — Prunus persica
PEANUT — Arachis hypogaea
PEAR — Pyrus communis
PINEAPPLE — Ananas comosus
PLUM — Prunus domestica
POMEGRANATE — Punica granatum
SWEET POTATO — Ipomoea batatus
SYCAMORE — Acer pseudoplatanus

Index

MORE ABOUT PENGUINS
AND PELICANS

Penguinews, which appears every month, contains details of all the new books issued by Penguins as they are published. From time to time it is supplemented by the *Penguin Stock List*, which is our list of almost 5,000 titles.

A specimen copy of *Penguinews* will be sent to you free on request. Please write to Dept EP, Penguin Books Ltd, Harmondsworth, Middlesex, for your copy.

In the U.S.A.: For a complete list of books available from Penguins in the United States write to Dept CS, Penguin Books, 625 Madison Avenue, New York, New York 10022.

In Canada: For a complete list of books available from Penguins in Canada write to Penguin Books Canada Ltd, 2801 John Street, Markham, Ontario L3R 1B4.